BIBLE HISTORY
WORKBOOK

—With Answer Key—

BIBLE HISTORY WORKBOOK

—With Answer Key—

By

Marie Ignatz

Based on the text by
Fr. George Johnson, Ph.D., Fr. Jerome D. Hannan, D.D.
and Sister M. Dominica, O.S.U., Ph.D.

TAN BOOKS AND PUBLISHERS, INC.
Rockford, Illinois 61105

Copyright © 2001 by TAN Books and Publishers, Inc.

ISBN 978-0-89555-703-2

Cover illustration: "Christ and the Doctors in the Temple," by Heinrich Hofmann. (Original at Riverside Church, New York).

Printed and bound in the United States of America.

TAN BOOKS AND PUBLISHERS, INC.
P.O. Box 424
Rockford, Illinois 61105
2001

"And Jesus coming, spoke to them, saying: All power is given to me in heaven and in earth. Going therefore, teach ye all nations; baptizing them in the name of the Father and of the Son, and of the Holy Ghost. Teaching them to observe all things whatsoever I have commanded you: and behold I am with you all days, even to the consummation of the world."

—*Matthew* 28:18-20

CONTENTS

𝕿𝖍𝖊 𝕺𝖑𝖉 𝕿𝖊𝖘𝖙𝖆𝖒𝖊𝖓𝖙

The New Testament

— Unit Six —
How Christ Prepared to Redeem the World

— Unit Seven —
How Christ Taught, Worked Miracles and Founded the Church

— Unit Eight —
How Christ Redeemed the World and Returned to Heaven

Perfect Score: 100   **Score:** _____

Completion — Part 1

Directions: Complete and make each statement true and accurate by writing one or more words on each blank line. Each blank is worth 2 points. 50 possible points.

1. God created us to know, love and _____ Him in this world and

   be happy with Him forever in the next.

2. Our most important lessons in life are the ones that help us to know God because then we will grow in our love for Him and we will want to do His holy

   _____ .

3. Since God created the world, the beautiful things in it like the stars and the

   flowers tell us that God is _____ .

4. The powerful things which God created show that God is

   _____ .

5. Our parents and friends who are kind and take care of us show that God,

   our Father in Heaven, _____ and cares for us.

6. Sometimes we make the mistake of giving to God's creations the honor which is

   due to _____ alone.

7. So that we have a better idea how to love and serve Him, God desires us to

   know _____ truths which are not in the "book of nature" because they are above nature.

8. God has given us the book, the _____ , so that we could learn of things that we otherwise would never know.

9. Truths that we know are true because God has told us they are true, even

   though we may not understand them, are called _____ .

10. The help that God gave to the writers of the Bible so that they could not make any mistakes when writing is called _____ .

11. Some of the writers of the Bible were Christ's apostles and _____ who were inspired by God to write down the things which He had said and done.

12. After the last apostle died, no one was ever given the gift of _____ again, since God had left us all the truths that we needed to know in order to enter the Kingdom of Heaven.

13. Christ founded His Church to guard and explain the _____ which He revealed, and since He promised to be with His Church until the end of _____ , she cannot make a mistake when she tells us what we need to believe and do.

14. We call the Church _____ because she cannot make a mistake when she tells us what we must believe and do.

15. The Bible is divided into two parts: the _____ , which is made up of forty-five books, and the _____ , which is made up of twenty-seven books.

16. The word testament means an agreement, or _____ , and sometimes the Bible uses the word _____ instead of testament.

17. The Old Testament gives us an account of how God promised us a _____ to save us from our _____ and of how He chose the Jews to prepare the world for His coming.

18. The New Testament shows how God's promise was _____ in Our Lord Jesus Christ and His Church.

19. The Bible's historical books tell the past, the moral books give us rules of conduct and tell how we should live, and the _____ books foretell certain things that will happen in the future.

20. Most of the Bible's books are written in _____ , not poetry.

21. The apostles told people about some of the other things which Jesus did that were not written down, and this passing down of truths by word of mouth is called _____ .

Completion — Part 2

Directions: Is each of these books of the Bible in the Old Testament or in the New Testament? (Note: The Books of the Bible are usually called simply by the main word of their title. For example, the Epistle to the Philippians is called simply Philippians.) Put either OT or NT in each blank. Each blank is worth 2 points. 50 possible points.

1. _____ Hebrews

2. _____ Romans

3. _____ Deuteronomy

4. _____ Matthew

5. _____ Job

6. _____ Luke

7. _____ Isaias

8. _____ Jeremias

9. _____ I and II Machabees

10. _____ Genesis

11. _____ Daniel

12. _____ Psalms

13. _____ John (Gospel)

14. _____ John (3 Epistles)

15. _____ I and II Corinthians

16. _____ Judith

17. _____ Exodus

18. _____ Galatians

19. _____ Leviticus

20. _____ Zacharias

21. _____ I and II Timothy

22. _____ Acts of the Apostles

23. _____ The Apocalypse

24. _____ Esther

25. _____ Ecclesiasticus

The Old Testament

| Unit One Section I | **I. The Story of the Creation** | Text Pages 3-14 |

Perfect Score: 100   Score: _____

Completion

Directions: Complete and make each statement true and accurate by writing one or more words on each blank line. Each blank is worth 1 point. 80 possible points.

1. From all eternity God _____ .

2. God always was and never had a _____ .

3. The Father, Son and the Holy Ghost are one _____ , and are

   _____ to each other in all things.

4. There is no _____ that God does not know, no

   _____ that He does not possess, no _____

   that He does not enjoy.

5. God created Heaven and earth out of _____ . He created them

   not because He _____ them, but so that creatures could share

   in His _____ and glory.

6. There are _____ choirs, or kinds, of angels.

7. The lowest classes of angels are the Angels and the _____ ,

   while the highest classes of angels are the _____ and

   _____ .

8. Each one of us has a _____ Angel to watch over us and protect us.

9. Before they could enjoy Heaven, God's newly created angels had to pass a test in which they proved that they loved _____ more than _____ .

10. The leader of the proud angels who refused to obey God was _____ , one of the highest angels that God had created.

11. The leader of the good angels in the great battle in Heaven was _____ .

12. After the great battle in Heaven between the good angels and the bad angels, Lucifer was henceforth known as _____, or the devil.

13. All hope of ever entering the Kingdom of _____ has been taken away from the fallen angels.

14. The Book of _____ tells us that all things were created by God.

15. The first book of the Bible divides up the whole work of creation into _____ days.

16. The word day, as it is used in the Bible does not necessarily mean a period of _____ hours.

17. The beginning of the first book of the Bible says "In the _____ God created _____ and _____ . And the earth was _____ and _____ ."

18. On the first day, God called the light _____ and the darkness _____ .

19. God created the dry land on the _____ day and called it _____ , and the gathering of the waters together He called _____ .

20. "And He blessed the _____ day, and _____ it, because in it He had rested from all His work."

21. God created man according to His own _____ and
    _____ .

22. God made man out of the _____ of the earth, and breathed
    into his face the breath of _____ .

23. God gave man dominion over "the _____ of the sea, and
    the _____ of the air, and the beasts, and the whole
    _____ , and every creeping _____ that
    moveth upon the earth."

24. The name Adam means _____ .

25. God made a wonderful garden called _____ , or The Garden of
    _____ , and gave it to Adam as his home.

26. All the beasts of the earth and the fowls of the air were brought to Adam to have
    him give them a _____ .

27. While Adam slept, God took one of his_____ and made a
    _____ .

28. When God brought Eve to Adam, Adam said, "This is _____ of
    my bones and _____ of my flesh."

29. The name Eve means _____ of all the
    _____ .

30. God clothed the souls of Adam and Eve with _____ , which
    made them become _____ and pleasing in His sight and gave
    them the right to be happy with Him for all _____ .

31. God told Adam and Eve that if they loved and obeyed Him, they would
    never _____ , but would finally be taken up into
    _____ .

32. Satan _____ Adam and Eve because he saw their happiness
    and how much God _____ them.

33. Adam and Eve were forbidden by God to eat of the tree of Knowledge of _____ and _____ .

34. The serpent said, "_____ knows that if you eat of the fruit of that tree, your eyes shall be _____ and you shall be as _____ ."

35. Adam blamed _____ for his sin of disobedience to God, and Eve blamed _____ .

36. God said to the serpent, "I will put enmities between thee and the _____ , and between thy _____ and her seed; she shall crush thy _____ ."

37. As punishment for sin, God told Adam, "In the sweat of thy _____ thou shalt earn thy _____ till thou return to the _____ ."

38. God said to Adam, "For dust thou art and into _____ thou shalt return."

39. After their sin, Adam and Eve were clothed in garments of _____ .

40. A _____ with a flaming _____ was stationed outside the Garden of Paradise to guard it and make sure Adam and Eve could not return to it.

41. The sin that Adam and Eve have passed down through the generations is called _____ Sin.

42. The only human being who was preserved from sin is the _____ .

Matching

Directions: In each blank, write the letter of the phrase that correctly identifies that person, group, place or thing. Each blank is worth 2 points. 20 possible points.

1. ___ Blessed Virgin Mary

2. ___ Paradise

3. ___ Michael

4. ___ Adam

5. ___ third day

6. ___ Cherubim

7. ___ Lucifer

8. ___ Eve

9. ___ first day

10. ___ Angels and Archangels

A) Mother of All the Living
B) dry land was created
C) Earthborn
D) leader of good Angels
E) lowest of the choirs of Angels

F) preserved from Original Sin
G) day and night were made
H) Garden of Eden

I) leader of the proud and disobedient Angels
J) guarded Garden of Paradise after the first sin

BIBLE HISTORY — WORKBOOK

Unit One
Section II

II. The Descendants of Adam and Eve

Text
Pages
15-18

Perfect Score: 100   Score: _____

Completion

Directions: Complete and make each statement true and accurate by writing one or more words on each blank line. Each blank is worth 2 points. 80 possible points.

1. God said to Adam, "In the _____ of thy face thou shalt eat thy _____," but also he promised that someday a _____ would crush the serpent's head and that God would save them from the effects of their _____ .

2. Adam and Eve and their children _____ God by giving Him back some of His gifts. They _____ the gifts up so they could never be given to anyone except to God. This type of offering we call a _____ .

3. Cain made his living from the _____ of the _____ , the trees and the vines, while Abel was a _____ .

4. God was pleased with _____ sacrifice, but with _____ He was displeased because he did not give his gift with a good _____ .

5. Cain killed _____ . After God asked Cain where his _____ was, Cain replied, "I know not. Am I my brother's _____ ?"

6. God said to Cain, "The _____ of thy brother's _____ crieth to Me from the _____ . _____ shalt thou be upon the earth."

7. Cain said, "My _____ is so great that I can never

be _____. Anyone that _____ me shall

_____ me."

8. God said, "But whosoever shall kill Cain, shall be punished

_____."

9. God put a _____ upon Cain so that whoever

_____ him would not _____ him.

10. After the death of Abel, God gave Adam another son named

_____, who was _____ to God.

11. Jabel was the father of such as dwell in _____, and of

_____."

12. _____ was "the father of them that play upon the harp and

the organs."

13. _____ was "a hammerer and _____

in every work of _____ and _____."

14. From Seth was descended _____, who

"_____ with God and was seen no more, because God

_____ him."

Matching

Directions: In each blank, write the letter of the phrase that correctly identifies
that person, group, place or thing. Each blank is worth 2 points. 20 possible points.

1. ___ Cain
2. ___ fruits of the fields
3. ___ Seth
4. ___ Henoch
5. ___ Lamech

6. ___ Abel
7. ___ burnt offering to God
8. ___ Adam
9. ___ Jabel
10. ___ lamb

A) sacrifice
B) son given to Adam after Abel
C) sacrifice given to God by Abel
D) vengeful son of Cain
E) shepherd
F) fugitive and vagabond
G) father of herdsmen
H) descendant of Seth
I) sacrifice of Cain
J) father of Cain and Abel

BIBLE HISTORY — WORKBOOK

Unit One
Section III

III. The Great Flood

Text
Pages
19-30

Perfect Score: 100   Score: _____

Completion

Directions: Complete and make each statement true and accurate by writing one or more words on each blank line. Each blank is worth 2 points. 80 possible points.

1. Most of the descendants of Adam and Eve were _____ ,

   _____ and _____ .

2. Noe's three sons who loved and served God were _____ ,

   _____ and _____ .

3. God told Noe that He would send a _____ to destroy the

   people and the _____ .

4. The ark was _____ feet long, _____
   feet wide and 45 feet high.

5. After the ark was finished, it rained for _____ days and

   _____ nights.

6. The second _____ Noe sent out returned carrying an

   _____ .

7. God made the _____ as a sign of his promise to Noe never

   again to _____ the earth by a flood.

8. Noe showed his gratitude to God by building an _____

   and offering a _____ of fowl and cattle.

9. Sem and _____ covered their father Noe with a

   _____ when he had drunk too much wine.

10. Noe _____ Cham, saying he would always be the

    _____ of his brothers.

11. Many years later, people said, "Let us make a city and a _____ , the top whereof may reach to _____ ."

12. God punished the people for building the tower by making the one _____ which the families had used up to this time into many different _____ .

13. The city from which the Lord scattered the people was called _____ .

14. The two great rivers that flowed through Babylon were the _____ and the _____ .

15. The method of writing done by pressing a wedge-shaped pencil into soft _____ and then baking it is called _____ .

16. During this time _____ the _____ united all the cities of the land to form one empire.

17. The " _____ of _____ " is the oldest code of laws in the world.

18. The warlike Chanaanites conquered the _____ on their east, but were never able to conquer the _____ on their west.

19. The _____ sent colonies into Palestine, and it is to them that the name Chanaanite is usually given.

20. The Hittites in Palestine were idolators who worshiped the false gods _____ and _____ .

Matching

Directions: In each blank, write the letter of the phrase that correctly identifies that person, group, place or thing. Each blank is worth 2 points. 20 possible points.

1. ___ Sargon the First

2. ___ Scythians, Medes, Greeks, Thracians

3. ___ Babel

4. ___ Cham

5. ___ Hittites

6. ___ Semites

7. ___ Hammurabi

8. ___ northern cities in Land of Senaar

9. ___ On

10. ___ pharao

A) Chanaanites' greatest King
B) servant of his brothers
C) later known as Assyrians

D) idolators
E) King of Egypt
F) Heliopolis
G) first great emperor
H) confusion

I) descendants of Sem
J) descendants of Japheth

BIBLE HISTORY — WORKBOOK

How God Founded the Nation from which the Redeemer of the World Came

Unit Two Section I	**I. Abraham, the Father of the Chosen People**	Text Pages 33-49

Perfect Score: 100 Score: _____

Completion

Directions: Complete and make each statement true and accurate by writing one or more words on each blank line. Each blank is worth 2 points. 80 possible points.

1. Abram was the son of _____, who lived in _____ , a city of Chaldea.

2. At the Lord's command, Abram took his wife _____, Lot, and their servants and flocks to the Land of _____ .

3. When quarrels arose between Abram's herdsmen and Lot's herdsmen, Lot chose to move to the land near the _____ , and he lived in the city of _____ .

4. Abram and his league numbering 318 attacked _____ , the King of _____ , to rescue Lot and the other captives.

5. After the battle, _____ , who was a _____ and priest at the same time, visited Abram and blessed him.

6. _____ is an image of Our Lord because he offered a sacrifice of _____ and _____ .

7. The 109th Psalm foretells that the _____ would be a great _____ and a great King.

8. God said to Abram, "Look up to heaven and _____ the _____ if thou canst. So shall thy _____ be."

9. Following Sarai's advice, Abram took the servant _____ as his wife, and God gave them a son named _____ .

10. The Angel of God told Agar regarding her son: "He shall be a _____ man. His hand will be _____ against all men, and all men's hands against him; and he shall pitch his _____ over against all his brethren."

11. God changed Abram's name to _____ and Sarai's name to _____ .

12. God told Abraham that his descendants would live in a land of strangers who would make _____ of them and afflict them for several years.

13. Abraham realized that the stranger who told him that Sara would have a son was _____ and that the others were _____ .

14. Since there were not even ten just men in the cities of _____ and _____ , these cities were destroyed by fire and brimstone.

15. Lot's wife turned into a statue of _____ because of her disobedience.

16. Isaac was born when Abraham was _____ years old and Sara was _____ years old.

17. Ismael and Agar were sent away because Sara did not want Ismael to be an _____ with Isaac.

18. The Lord commanded Abraham to offer his only _____ as a sacrifice; then, because of Abraham's faithfulness, an Angel of the Lord stopped him, and Abraham offered a _____ as a sacrifice instead.

19. An angel repeated God's promise to Abraham: "Thy _____ shall be as numerous as the stars in the heavens and as grains of sand on the seashore, and in your children shall all nations of the earth be blessed, because thou hast _____ my voice."

20. Abraham's servant Eliezar brought back _____ to be the bride for Isaac after she had offered to draw water from a well for Eliezar and his _____ .

Matching

Directions: In each blank, write the letter of the phrase that correctly identifies that person, group, place or thing. Each blank is worth 2 points. 20 possible points.

1. ___ Chodorlahomor

2. ___ Isaac

3. ___ Esau

4. ___ Abraham

5. ___ Abraham's sacrifice

6. ___ Melchisedech's sacrifice

7. ___ Sara

8. ___ turned to salt

9. ___ Melchisedech

10. ___ Rebecca

A) "princess"
B) Lot's wife
C) King of Salem
D) daughter of Bathuel

E) King of Babylonia
F) ram
G) heir of Abraham
H) bread and wine

I) "father of many nations"
J) married Ismael's daughter

BIBLE HISTORY — WORKBOOK

Unit Two
Section II

II. God's Great
Favors to Jacob

Text
Pages
50-61

Perfect Score: 100   Score: _____

Completion

Directions: Complete and make each statement true and accurate by writing one or more words on each blank line. Each blank is worth 2 points. 80 possible points.

1. God had told Rebecca that her _____ son would be greater

   than her _____ son.

2. Esau sold his _____ to Jacob by exchanging it for bread and a pottage of lentils.

3. Isaac told _____ to take something in the

   _____ and prepare a meal for him so that Isaac could

   _____ him before he died.

4. Rebecca covered Jacob's bare neck and hands with the little

   _____ of the two _____ that she had cooked for Isaac.

5. Isaac said to Jacob: "The voice indeed is the voice of _____ ,

   but the hands are the hands of _____ ." Isaac then blessed

   _____

6. Isaac took pity upon Esau and blessed him, saying, "Thou shalt live by the

   _____ and shalt _____ thy brother. And the time shall come when thou shalt shake off and loose his

   _____ from thy neck."

7. Isaac and Rebecca did not want Jacob to marry a Hittite woman, and Isaac

   told him, "Take not a wife from the stock of _____ ."

8. Rebecca suffered for her part in deceiving her husband. Her son _____ refused to have anything to do with her, and she never saw her other son _____ again.

9. On his journey to Haran, Jacob dreamt of a _____ reaching from earth to Heaven.

10. God told Jacob through a dream, "The land on which thou _____ I will give to thee and thy descendants. And they shall be as the _____ of the earth, and in thee and them all the tribes of the earth shall be _____."

11. Jacob worked for Laban for _____ years so that he could marry _____ , but Laban deceived Jacob and forced him to marry _____ instead.

12. Jacob agreed to work _____ more years in order to marry _____ , and six years after that to receive a share of the flocks.

13. After Jacob and Laban had separated, they formed a heap of stones, ate over it and solemnly agreed never to pass that spot to _____ each other's _____ .

14. When Jacob heard that _____ was coming to meet him with _____ hundred men, he divided his company into two groups, hoping that at least one group would escape.

15. After Jacob wrestled with the stranger, he said, "I will not let thee go unless thou _____ me," because the stranger was an _____ .

16. The stranger told Jacob that his name would no longer be Jacob, but _____ , which means _____ against God.

17. After the encounter with the stranger, Jacob said, "I have seen _____ face to face and my soul hath been _____."

18. At Bethel, Jacob built an _____ and offered

_____ to God.

19. In Bethlehem, Jacob's youngest son, _____ , was born, and Rachael his wife died.

20. After Isaac's death, Jacob became the _____ , or father of a great nation.

Matching

Directions: In each blank, write the letter of the phrase that correctly identifies that person, group, place or thing. Each blank is worth 2 points. 20 possible points.

1. ___ Mambre

2. ___ Dina

3. ___ Galaad

4. ___ Basemath

5. ___ Phanuel

6. ___ Lia

7. ___ Bethel

8. ___ Israel

9. ___ Rachel

10. ___ Laban

A) House of God
B) place where Jacob wrestled stranger
C) Jacob's second wife
D) wife of Esau

E) strong against God
F) Rachel's father
G) daughter of Jacob and Lia
H) burial cave

I) wife Jacob married first
J) The Witness Heap

BIBLE HISTORY — WORKBOOK

Unit Two
Section III

**III. The Children of
Israel in Egypt**

Text
Pages
62-80

Perfect Score: 100   Score: _____

Completion

Directions: Complete and make each statement true and accurate by writing one or more words on each blank line. Each blank is worth 1 point. 80 possible points.

1. Joseph's brothers were jealous of him because their father gave him a

   _____ of many _____ .

2. Joseph had a dream that his brothers' sheaves _____ down before his own sheaf.

3. Joseph said to his brothers, "I saw in a dream, as it were,

   the _____ , and the _____ , and

   _____ stars worshipping me."

4. When the other brothers wanted to kill Joseph, the oldest,

   _____ , tried to save Joseph's life and suggested that the

   brothers throw him into a _____ .

5. Joseph's brothers dipped his _____ in the blood of a kid so that

   Jacob would believe that he had been killed by a _____ .

6. Jacob's brothers sold him to some merchants on their way to

   _____ .

7. The merchants sold Joseph to _____ , the chief captain of
   Pharao's army, where he placed Joseph in charge of the house.

8. Putiphar's _____ falsely accused Joseph of

   _____ because he would not do wrong to please her.

9. The three _____ in the butler's dream referred to the three

   days before _____ accepted him back into his palace.

10. The three _____ in the baker's dream referred to the three days before which Pharao would cut off his head.

11. The _____ forgot Joseph and what Joseph had done for him until _____ years later, when Pharao needed someone to explain his _____ .

12. Joseph told the Pharao that the power to interpret dreams comes from _____ .

13. The seven beautiful cows and seven full ears of _____ in Pharao's dreams represented seven years of _____ , while the seven _____ cows and seven thin ears represented seven years of _____ .

14. Pharao said to Joseph, "Thou shalt be over my _____ ." Only _____ would be above Joseph.

15. Pharao appointed Joseph to be _____ over all of _____ and declared that the people should bow their _____ before him.

16. Egypt's fertility depended upon the overflow of the _____ , which could reach no lower than _____ feet or the crops would fail, resulting in a _____ .

17. Joseph married _____ 's daughter, _____ .

18. Since the father of Joseph's wife was a _____ , a position which belonged to one of the highest classes among the Egyptians, Joseph's marriage gave him a high _____ standing.

19. Joseph was in charge of storing up _____ of the grain produced during the seven years of _____ .

20. When the famine spread to the Land of _____ , Jacob sent his sons to buy grain in _____ , but he kept the youngest son, _____ , at home.

21. When Joseph's brothers first came to him, he accused them of being

    _____ .

22. Joseph told his brothers that their brother _____ would
    not be released from prison until they brought to him the

    _____ whom they had left home.

23. When Joseph heard his brothers tell each other that they deserved to be

    punished for what they had done to him, he wept for _____

    because he knew that they had _____ of their sin.

24. Joseph instructed the servants to put the _____ which his

    brothers had _____ into the mouths of their sacks of grain.

25. When Jacob's family needed grain the second time, he only allowed his son

    _____ to go with the brothers after _____
    promised that no harm would come to him.

26. Joseph commanded his servants to put his _____ into the

    mouth of _____ 's sack.

27. Joseph's brothers were so sure they did not have what they were accused of

    stealing that they were ready to become Joseph's _____
    if it were found in their sacks, and they were willing that the one who had it

    should be put to _____ .

28. _____ offered himself to be Joseph's slave in

    _____ 's place.

29. Joseph told his brothers that it was _____ 's will that he had

    been sent to _____ to save his family from

    _____ .

30. Pharao gave presents to Joseph's brothers, especially to

    _____ , and to Jacob he gave _____

    and _____ pieces of silver.

31. When Jacob was reunited with Joseph, he said, "Now shall I

_____ with _____ , because I have seen

thy _____ and leave thee _____ ."

32. Pharao gave Jacob the land of _____ .

33. When Joseph heard that his father was sick, he took his sons

_____ and _____ to Jacob, who blessed

them.

34. Jacob prophesied, "The scepter shall not be taken away from

_____ . . . till He come that is to be sent, and He shall be the

_____ of _____ ."

35. Jacob prophesied, "_____ is a growing son, a growing son and

_____ to behold. . . ." The Church uses these words in the

Mass for the Feast of _____ .

36. When Jacob died, his body was carried in a great _____ to the

Land of _____ .

37. Joseph prophesied that his father's race would leave the land of

_____ , and he ordered that his _____

be taken with them when they would go.

Matching

Directions: In each blank, write the letter of the phrase that correctly identifies that person, group, place or thing. Each blank is worth 2 points. 20 possible points.

1. ___ Manasses

2. ___ Simeon

3. ___ land where Jacob was
        buried

4. ___ Ephraim

5. ___ Putiphare

6. ___ Ruben

7. ___ baker

8. ___ butler

9. ___ Aseneth

10. ___ land Pharao gave to
         Jacob

A) priest of Heliopolis
B) Land of Chanaan
C) youngest son of Joseph
D) Joseph's wife

E) released from prison on Pharao's birthday
F) land of Gessen
G) Joseph's brother who remained in prison

H) oldest son of Joseph
I) oldest son of Jacob
J) put to death by Pharao

BIBLE HISTORY — WORKBOOK

Unit Three
Section I

I. The Departure of the Israelites from Egypt

Text Pages 83-105

Perfect Score: 100   Score: _____

Completion

Directions: Complete and make each statement true and accurate by writing one or more words on each blank line. Each blank is worth 1 point. 80 possible points.

1. Jacob's descendants were called _____ .

2. Lot's and Esau's descendants led a _____ life in Chanaan, while the Israelites grew in prosperity in Egypt.

3. Many of the Chosen People had fallen into _____ and the vices of the Egyptians during their time of freedom, but when they were turned into slaves, they turned their thoughts to _____ .

4. So that the Jews did not revolt against him, Pharao ordered every little Jewish _____ be killed.

5. Moses' mother made a wicker basket, covered it with _____ and put it in the _____ near the _____ River.

6. _____ 's daughter found the basket with Moses in it, and _____ , Moses' sister, asked the princess if she wanted a _____ woman to nurse him.

7. When he was older, Moses lived in the _____ and was educated as a _____ .

8. It pained Moses to see how the _____ , his own people, were treated.

9. One day, when Moses saw an Egyptian _____ mistreat an Israelite, he _____ him.

10. Since Pharao ordered that Moses be put to death, Moses escaped to _____ , which is in the region of _____ .

11. Moses defended the daughters of _____ from some shepherds and eventually married the daughter named _____ .

12. Moses lived with Jethro for _____ years.

13. Moses was tending flocks when he saw a _____ in flames that did not _____ up.

14. God told Moses, "Put off the _____ from thy _____ , for the place where thou standest is _____ ground. I am the God of _____ , the God of _____ , and the God of _____ ."

15. God told Moses that he would bring His people out of Egypt to a land flowing with _____ and _____ .

16. As a sign that God had sent him, Moses, after leading God's people out of Egypt, would offer a _____ to God upon the same mountain upon which Moses first heard God speak to him from the bush.

17. When Moses asked God what he should tell the people God's name was, God answered, "I am WHO _____ . Tell them that He WHO _____ hath sent thee."

18. In order to prove to the people that Moses was to be their leader, God gave Moses the power to turn his rod into a _____ .

19. When Moses put his hand into his bosom and then drew it out again at the Lord's command, it was covered with _____ and was white as snow.

20. The third sign that God gave Moses for the people was the power to turn water from the river into _____ .

21. Moses protested that he was slow of speech, so God appointed _____ to speak for him.

22. God had spoken to Moses and given him signs on Mount _____ .

23. Moses and his brothers asked Pharao to let the Israelites take a _____ days' journey into the _____ to offer sacrifice to God.

24. To punish the Israelites for Moses and his brother's request, the Israelites were forced to gather _____ to hold the clay together.

25. The serpent from Aaron's rod _____ the serpents formed from the rods that belonged to Pharao's magicians.

26. After the first plague, in which the river water was turned to blood, Pharao would not let the Children of Israel leave Egypt because his heart was _____ .

27. At the second plague, the magicians of Pharao were also able to cause _____ to come upon the land, but they were not able to imitate the third plague, the plague of _____ .

28. After the third plague, the magicians told Pharao, "This is the _____ of God."

29. Moses refused to offer sacrifice to God in Egypt since the Egyptians would have _____ the Israelites for killing the animals which the Egyptians worshiped.

30. In the fifth plague, all the animals except those in _____ were afflicted with disease and death.

31. Even after the sixth plague, when the people and animals were plagued with _____ , and even after Moses threatened a seventh plague, a plague of _____ , Pharao did not obey God's word.

32. At the threat of the plague of locusts, Pharao said that the Israelite _____ could go, but not the _____ and

_____ .

33. After the land was covered in _____ , Pharao told Moses and Aaron that all of the people could go, but that they had to leave their _____ behind. This was not acceptable because the people needed these as _____ for the sacrifice.

34. In obedience to God's command, the Israelites asked their Egyptian neighbors for gifts of _____ and _____ .

35. Moses told the Israelites to prepare a _____ without a blemish, and to sacrifice it on the _____ day of the month.

36. The Israelites were also instructed by Moses to sprinkle the posts of the house with the animal's _____ , and to eat its roasted flesh with _____ bread and _____ lettuce, and to eat in _____ , with staves in their hands, ready for a long journey, because it was the _____ of the Lord.

37. The destroying angel entered every Egyptian home and killed every _____ , but spared the Israelites because of the _____ of the lamb sprinkled on their door posts.

38. When the Israelites left Egypt, they remembered the promise their ancestors had made to _____ and took his remains with them.

39. The Lord led the Israelites by a pillar of _____ by day and a pillar of _____ by night.

40. God told Moses to stretch out his _____ over the _____ Sea, which divided the waters to let the Israelites pass through; and once they had crossed to the other shore, He gave Moses power to close the waters so that the Egyptians were drowned.

41. To feed the children of Israel, God sent them quail at night and a special bread in the morning that tasted like flour and honey which the Israelites called

_____ .

42. When the people were thirsty, God commanded Moses to strike a

_____ , and water gushed out of it.

43. During the Israelites' battle against the _____ , Moses prayed for victory, and the Israelites were successful as long as Moses held the

_____ of God up over his head.

44. Moses fulfilled God's prophecy when he built an _____ on the mountain in thanksgiving to God.

45. Moses appointed _____ to settle the people's disputes after he

had listened to the advice of _____ , who had brought with him Moses' wife and two sons.

Matching

Directions: In each blank, write the letter of the phrase that correctly identifies that person, group, place or thing. Each blank is worth 2 points. 20 possible points.

1. ___ fourth plague
2. ___ second plague
3. ___ land of Gessen
4. ___ Mara
5. ___ Jethro

6. ___ manna
7. ___ Mount Horeb
8. ___ Raphidim
9. ___ Mount Sinai
10. ___ ninth plague

A) Madian is in the region of this mountain
B) heavy dew covering the earth
C) mountain of burning bush
D) Moses' father-in-law
E) darkness
F) flies
G) bitterness
H) frogs
I) spared from plagues
J) battle with Amalecites

BIBLE HISTORY — WORKBOOK

Perfect Score: 100   Score: _____

Completion

Directions: Complete and make each statement true and accurate by writing one or more words on each blank line. Each blank is worth 1 point. 80 possible points.

1. After leaving Mount Horeb, the Israelites stayed for _____ years in a valley at the foot of Mount _____ .

2. Before giving His people the Ten Commandments, God promised them that if they were _____ to the law, He would make them His _____ People.

3. For _____ days, the people prepared for the law to be given them, and then God told Moses to draw a _____ line at the bottom of the mountain which the people could not pass under pain of _____ .

4. The second commandment is, "Thou shalt not take the _____ of the Lord thy God in _____ ."

5. After God spoke to the people amidst thunder and lightning, they said to Moses, "Speak thou to us and we shall _____ . Let not the Lord speak to us, or we shall _____ ."

6. God promised Moses that an _____ would lead the Israelites to the _____ Land.

7. The Israelites were ordered by God to drive out the inhabitants of _____ .

8. Moses poured _____ from a sacrifice on the altar and sprinkled the rest on the people and on the book he had written as a sign of the solemn _____ between God and His people.

9. Moses remained in the cloud on the mountain for _____ days and _____ nights.

10. Since Moses had been gone so long, the Israelites forced _____ to make a golden _____ for them to adore.

11. Moses was so angry at seeing the Israelites' false worship that he threw down and broke the tablets of _____ on which were written the Ten Commandments, and then burnt the _____ and beat it into powder.

12. After the Israelites' sin of idolatry, Moses cried out, "If any man be on the _____'s side, let him join with _____."

13. After Moses passed a sentence of death on those who had led the others into idolatry, the sons of _____ slew the guilty, whoever came in their way. _____ men were killed, and God forgave the rest because they did _____ .

14. Moses went up to the mountain again, remaining there for another _____ days and _____ nights, and God again wrote the _____ .

15. When Moses came down the mountain again, rays of light like _____ shone from his face. This frightened the Israelites, so he put a _____ over his face.

16. The _____ was a portable church that was easy to take apart and was _____ feet long, 15 feet wide and 15 feet high.

17. The _____ was the room where the Ark of the Covenant rested. It was separated by a curtain from the _____ or Holy Place, the other part of the Tabernacle.

18. The _____ of the Tabernacle was 150 feet long and _____ feet wide, with the Tabernacle at its west end and the Altar of _____ inside its entrance.

BIBLE HISTORY — WORKBOOK

19. The Brazen _____ was a bowl of brass where the priests purified themselves, washing their hands and feet before entering the Tabernacle.

20. The Ark contained the two tablets of the law, a vessel containing _____ , and later, the _____ of Aaron.

21. God spoke to Moses from a cloud resting over the _____ Seat, the golden cover of the _____ of the Covenant. This _____ was the only thing placed in the Holy of Holies.

22. At each end of the Table of Showbreads were _____ loaves of unleavened showbread, which were renewed every _____ as a constant offering of _____ to God.

23. The Altar of _____ was placed before the Holy of Holies, and the Altar of _____ was placed just inside the Court's entrance.

24. The _____-branched Candlestick that lit the Tabernacle's _____ was pure gold and weighed 130 pounds.

25. _____ and his sons were priests, and they alone could offer sacrifice to God.

26. The high priest's _____ , or outermost garment, was fastened by stones that had the names of the twelve _____ of Israel engraved on them.

27. Both the high priest and the priests wore the linen _____ on their heads, but that of the high priest had an inscription which read: _____ to the Lord.

28. Moses anointed _____ 's head with oil and _____ the hands of his two sons.

29. Because of their faithfulness to God at the time of the Golden Calf, the whole Tribe of _____ was appointed to help the priests.

30. The people placed their hands upon each of the Levites' heads as a sign that the nation was transferring to them the _____ to serve God in acts of public _____ .

31. The _____ sacrifices were those in which the fruits of the earth, or flour, dried corn and frankincense, along with oil and wine, were offered.

32. The _____ sacrifices were those in which certain animals without blemish were slain.

33. Sacrifices in which the entire victim was consumed by fire, as an act of adoration to acknowledge God's supreme dominion, were called _____ .

34. The _____ offering was the type of bloody sacrifice offered as an act of thanksgiving or _____ .

35. Sowing and reaping were forbidden during the _____ Year, every seventh year.

36. God appointed _____ days to remind the Israelites of the _____ they owed Him and of the great events in their history for which they owed Him gratitude.

37. The Day of _____ was the great day of public penance and was the one day that the high priest could enter the _____ .

38. On the Feast of the _____ in the month of _____ , the Israelites ate the Paschal _____ in their tents with _____ bread and bitter herbs, standing up and dressed in their traveling clothes to remind them of the night when God protected them from the destroying angel and led them out of Egypt.

39. The Feast of _____ was celebrated in thanksgiving for the harvest and commemorated the Israelites' receiving the Law on Mount _____ .

40. More sacrifices were offered during the seven days of the Feast of _____ than during any other feast.

41. On certain feast days the people were forbidden to do _____ work.

Matching

Directions: In each blank, write the letter of the phrase that correctly identifies that person, group, place or thing. Each blank is worth 2 points. 20 possible points.

1. ___ Sanctuary

2. ___ sin offerings

3. ___ Feast of the Pasch

4. ___ Mercy Seat

5. ___ Rational

6. ___ trespass offerings

7. ___ Showbread

8. ___ Azymes

9. ___ scapegoat

10. ___ golden calf

A) Passover
B) breastplate of high priest
C) Loaves of Proposition
D) "Holy Place"

E) unleavened bread
F) for venial sins
G) led into the wilderness
    on Day of Atonement

H) idol
I) for grievous sins
J) Propitiatory

BIBLE HISTORY — WORKBOOK

Perfect Score: 100   Score: _____

Completion

Directions: Complete and make each statement true and accurate by writing one or more words on each blank line. Each blank is worth 1 point. 80 possible points.

1. After Moses took the census, the _____ which had remained

   over the Tabernacle for _____ years ascended and moved in
   the direction in which the Israelites were to travel.

2. The _____ were at the head of the procession carrying the

   _____ .

3. After about _____ days of marching, the Israelites murmured

   against God, and He sent _____ down upon them to destroy

   some and to cause the rest to _____ .

4. One of the rebellions against Moses began because the Israelites were tired of

   eating _____ , so the Lord sent them a great number of

   _____ .

5. Even Aaron the high priest rebelled, and Miriam was punished with

   _____ for _____ days for her own rebellion
   during one of the revolts.

6. The Israelites stopped at _____ , where scouts were sent to

   explore the Land of _____ and then report back to the
   Israelites what they had seen.

7. The scouts told the people, "We came to the land to which thou didst send us, and in very truth it is a land flowing with _____ and _____ . . . . But the people that live there are very _____ , and they have great _____ , surrounded by strong _____ ."

8. Caleb said to the people, "Let us go up and _____ the land, for we shall be able to _____ it."

9. The unhappy Israelites told Moses they did not want him to be their leader and tried to elect a _____ who would lead them back to _____ .

10. The ten _____ were struck dead for causing the rebellion, but _____ and _____ were spared and were allowed to enter the _____ .

11. As punishment for the rebellion, the Israelites over _____ years old were made to linger in the desert until they _____ .

12. Some Israelites tried to enter Chanaan without Moses, but the _____ slew them and drove them back because _____ was not with them.

13. Others, including Core and _____ leaders, tried to perform the duties of the _____ , but the earth opened up and _____ them.

14. When some of the rebels tried to do harm to Moses and Aaron, they fled to the _____ , and God destroyed the rest of the rebels with a _____ .

15. During the time of peace, Aaron's rod _____ miraculously. This was a sign that his _____ placed him above all the other leaders except _____ .

16. God told Moses to take Aaron's rod and _____ to the rock before the people, and it would yield waters.

17. For a moment, Moses did not trust in God; he struck the _____ twice instead of doing as God had commanded; his punishment was that he was not allowed to enter the _____ .

18. After thirty-eight years in exile, the Israelites moved away from _____ and the desert of _____ .

19. Upon reaching Mount _____ , Aaron's priestly robes were taken and put upon his son _____ , who was to be the next high priest. Soon after, _____ died, and the people mourned for _____ days.

20. Since the people complained against Moses in the scorching _____ of _____ for bringing them out of Egypt, God put fiery _____ in their midst.

21. In answer to Moses' prayer, God instructed Moses, "Make a brazen _____ and set it up for a sign. Whoever, being _____ , shall look on it, shall _____ ."

22. The Israelites marched through the land of the _____ , taking possession of the _____ and of many of the towns.

23. The territory east of the Jordan was divided among the tribes of _____ , _____ and the half tribe of _____ .

24. Moses appointed _____ from the tribe of _____ to be the next civil and _____ leader of the Israelites.

25. Before his death, Moses went to the top of Mount _____ where God showed him the _____ ; he was _____ years old when he died.

26. Moses' _____ was hidden by God from the Israelites so that they would not _____ his body, since they were easily tempted to _____ .

27. On the way to _____ , Balaam's ass went to the side of the road to save Balaam from the _____ with the sword.

28. At King Balac's request, _____ attempted to _____ the Israelites _____ times, but each time his words turned into a _____ .

29. Balaam said to Balac, "Can I _____ anything else except what the Lord _____ ?"

30. Before Balaam returned home, he prophesied, "A _____ shall rise out of _____ and a _____ shall spring up from _____ . . . Out of Jacob shall He come that shall _____ ."

Matching

Directions: In each blank, write the letter of the phrase that correctly identifies that person, group, place or thing. Each blank is worth 2 points. 20 possible points.

1. ___ Miriam
2. ___ Cades
3. ___ Moses
4. ___ Eleazar
5. ___ Balac

6. ___ Core, Dathan, Abiron
7. ___ Mount Nebo
8. ___ Josue
9. ___ Mount Hor
10. ___ Land of Chanaan

A) King of Moabites
B) where Moses saw Promised Land
C) Moses' successor
D) grave hidden from Israelites
E) "land flowing with milk and honey"
F) on border of Chanaan
G) where Aaron died
H) buried at Cades
I) tried to perform priests' duties
J) Aaron's successor

IV. Josue, the Commander of the Israelites

Perfect Score: 100   Score: _____

Completion

Directions: Complete and make each statement true and accurate by writing one or more words on each blank line. Each blank is worth 1 point. 80 possible points.

1. With _____ and the _____ Sea on

   Chanaan's west and _____ on its east, Chanaan was almost

   the _____ of the ancient world.

2. The Bible describes the Land of Chanaan as "a good land of brooks and of

   waters and of _____ . . . wherein fruit trees and

   _____ and _____ yards grow—a land of

   oil and _____ ."

3. Chanaan was approximately the size of the U. S. state of

   _____ .

4. The region to the east of the Jordan was better for raising

   _____ and _____ than the region to its

   west.

5. Mount _____ is the only mountain along the coast of the

   Mediterranean, and the _____ is the most important river
   in this land.

6. The two seasons in Chanaan are the _____ season and the

   _____ season.

7. The most powerful tribe in Chanaan was that of the _____ ,

   who had reached the height of their power under King _____

   when living on the Island of _____ .

8. The Promised Land received the name _____ from the nation

of the _____ .

9. The Israelites learned how to work in _____ and may have

learned how to use the _____ , instead of picture writing, from
the Philistines.

10. The _____ were _____ people from Arabia
who caused problems for the Israelites.

11. After Sodom and Gomorrha were destroyed, _____ settled in

the country that bordered the east coast of the _____ Sea.

The _____ are descended from Lot's son Moab.

12. The Edomites worshiped _____ on hills called

"_____ Places" which tempted the Israelites away from

worshiping the one _____ God.

13. The prophet Abdias said to the Edomites, "'Though thou be exalted as an

_____ , and though thou set thy nest among the

_____ , thence will I bring thee down,' saith the Lord. 'I shall

destroy the _____ out of Edom, and _____

out of the mount of _____ . There shall be no remains of the

house of _____ , for the Lord hath spoken.'"

14. The Amorrhites formed two kingdoms: _____ as the northern

kingdom and _____ as the southern kingdom.

15. God told the Israelites to kill the _____ , "lest they teach

thee to do all the _____ which they have done to their God,
and thou shouldst sin against the Lord, thy God."

16. The Israelites' weapons were the short, pointed _____ , the

spear, the bow and arrow, and the _____ .

17. A woman named _____ hid the two spies which Josue

sent to the city of _____ and agreed to put a

_____ cord in her window to signal when the city was ready
to fall.

18. God commanded Josue to have the priests carry the Ark of the Covenant into

the _____ , and when they did, the course of the

_____ stopped and a _____ appeared.

19. A stone _____ was built in the middle of the Jordan to
commemorate their miraculous passage.

20. The Israelites celebrated the Feast of the Passover at _____ ,

where the _____ ceased to fall because they had finally
reached their destination.

21. An _____ of the Lord with a drawn _____
appeared to Josue and gave him instructions on how to take the city of Jericho.

22. _____ thousand Israelite soldiers marched around Jericho's

walls every day for _____ days.

23. On the _____ day, all the Israelites, with the priests carrying

the _____ of the _____ , marched around

the walls _____ times.

24. Then Josue shouted, " _____ , for the Lord hath delivered the

_____ to you."

25. The city walls fell at the sound of the seven _____
and the people shouting.

26. The Israelites were defeated in the city of Hai because of the

_____ of one of Josue's men named _____ ,

who had kept some of the _____ of Jericho for himself.

27. Josue's men defeated Hai in their second battle, with 5,000 men lying in

_____ behind the city.

28. Five cities, not including _____ , which had made a treaty with Josue, united to attack the Israelites.

29. Josue said, "Move not, O _____ , toward Gabaon, nor thou, O _____ , toward the valley of Ajalon" and God made them stand still until Josue's victory was complete.

30. Josue's third campaign was against the northern cities who were led by the King of _____ .

31. When the fighting was over, certain cities among the tribes were given to the _____ and _____ .

32. Three tribes had been given land across the river on the _____ shore of the Jordan, so they received Josue's blessing before they left.

33. Josue warned the Israelites against falling into _____ , and he set a _____ under an oak tree in the Court of the Tabernacle, which had been placed in _____ .

34. Josue spent the rest of his life in _____ .

35. _____ died shortly after Josue, and his son Phinees became the next _____ .

36. Joseph's bones were buried in _____ 's field at Sichem.

Matching

Directions: In each blank, write the letter of the phrase that correctly identifies that person, group, place or thing. Each blank is worth 2 points. 20 possible points.

1. ___ use of an alphabet

2. ___ use of picture writing

3. ___ Edomites

4. ___ Lebanon mountains

5. ___ Og

6. ___ Sehon

7. ___ Brook of Egypt

8. ___ Phinees

9. ___ Achan

10. ___ King Minos

A) Amorrhite King
   of Basan
B) was King of the
   Philistines
C) third high priest

D) to the south of
   Chanaan
E) Philistines
F) to the north of
   Chanaan

G) Amorrhite King of
   Gallad
H) descendants of Esau
I) Egyptians
J) kept plunder of Jericho

BIBLE HISTORY — WORKBOOK

Unit Three
Section V

V. The Israelites in the Promised Land

Text
Pages
154-166

Perfect Score: 100

Score: _____

Completion

Directions: Complete and make each statement true and accurate by writing one or more words on each blank line. Each blank is worth 2 points. 80 possible points.

1. The Israelites' form of government in the Promised Land was _____ , with each family or tribe having its own head.

2. Many of the Israelites forgot God's command for them to conquer all the territory and drive out the _____ inhabitants.

3. The strongest and most courageous man who the tribes chose to lead them in times of trouble was called a _____ .

4. There are fifteen _____ named in the Bible.

5. Gedeon overthrew the _____ that his father built to the false god _____ and erected one to the true God in its place.

6. Gedeon was called by God to lead the fight against the _____ .

7. The first sign Gedeon asked of God was that the fleece be covered with _____ and the ground around it be _____ .

8. The second sign Gedeon asked of God was that the fleece be _____ and the ground around it be wet with _____ .

9. By watching the way ten thousand men drank the water from the river, Gedeon chose _____ hundred men to be his army.

10. The Israelites forgot that God was their King and they tried to make _____ their king, who said, "I will not rule over you, neither shall my son rule over you, but the _____ shall rule over you."

11. The Israelites did not go to _____ to worship at the Tabernacle

    and fell into _____ after Gedeon's death.

12. Samson did not have an _____ like the other Judges because

    he depended upon the _____ that God had given him.

13. The Philistines burned Samson's _____'s house, and Samson's
    wife died.

14. When Samson was in Gaza, he carried the _____ of the city to
    a neighboring hill.

15. Samson revealed the secret of his strength to the Philistine woman

    _____ , telling her that if his _____ were

    cut, his strength would leave him.

16. When Samson's _____ had grown long again, he called upon

    the Lord to give him strength, and then he shook the _____ of
    the banquet hall, killing both the Philistines and himself.

17. When Elcana and Anna left their son Samuel with the high priest, Anna said,

    "I have _____ him to the Lord all the days of his life."

18. _____ and _____ robbed the people who
    came to offer sacrifice, and their father, Heli, neglected to punish them as they
    deserved.

19. The third time Samuel heard a voice calling him during the night, he answered,

    "Speak, Lord, for Thy _____ heareth."

20. The Lord told Samuel that He would punish Heli for his _____
    and his sons for their sins.

21. The _____ killed Heli's two sons in battle and captured the

    _____ .

22. Upon hearing the outcome of this battle against the Philistines,

    _____ fell from his chair and died.

23. The Ark of the Covenant was placed in the temple of the Philistine false god, _____ ; the statue of this false god was found on its face before the Ark.

24. In punishment for taking the Ark, the Philistine city of Azotus suffered from a plague of _____ , and other cities suffered from _____ .

25. The Ark was put on a cart led by two _____ , who carried it to the fields of a _____ in Bethsames.

26. _____ thousand people died in punishment for their irreverence toward the Ark.

27. Samuel urged the Israelites to return to the _____ of God.

28. At Masphath, Samuel had a sacrifice offered to God to obtain victory, and the Israelites defeated the _____ .

Matching

Directions: In each blank, write the letter of the phrase that correctly identifies that person, group, place or thing. Each blank is worth 2 points. 20 possible points.

1. ___ Cariathiarim
2. ___ Samuel
3. ___ Heli
4. ___ Ophni and Phinees
5. ___ Samson

6. ___ Madianites
7. ___ Philistines
8. ___ Elcana
9. ___ Judges
10. ___ Gedeon

A) waged war upon Israelites for 7 years
B) an Angel foretold his birth
C) waged war upon Israelites for 40 years

D) ruled in times of trouble
E) grew up in the Tabernacle
F) city known for its holiness

G) "O most valiant of men"
H) high priest
I) father of Samuel
J) wicked priests

Unit Three
Section VI

VI. The Story of Ruth

Text
Pages
167-170

Perfect Score: 100   Score: _____

Completion

Directions: Complete and make each statement true and accurate by writing one or more words on each blank line. Each blank is worth 2 points. 80 possible points.

1. Due to a _____ , Elimech left _____ , took his wife _____ and two sons and moved to the country of _____ .

2. Noemi's sons married _____ women, one named _____ and the other named _____ .

3. Noemi's sons died after _____ years. Her husband Emilech had already died.

4. The three widows set out for _____ 's home because she heard that God had been good to His people in _____ .

5. Noemi said to her daughters-in-law, "Go, return each to your _____ 's house, and may God have _____ upon you for all you have done for our _____ ones and for myself."

6. Ruth said to Noemi, "Thy _____ shall be my _____ , and thy _____ my _____ . Only _____ shall separate me from thee."

7. An Israelite law said that when a man died leaving behind a widow and no children, his nearest _____ could marry the widow and raise children in his stead.

8. Ruth went into the field of _____ to _____ among the ears of grain.

9. The Law of _____ forbade the owner of a field to go over it a _____ time; it commanded that the _____ left on the ground be left for the _____ .

10. Ruth _____ in the field until _____ , made the grain into _____ and brought it to _____ .

11. _____ was pleased to see Ruth gleaning in his field; he had heard of the _____ she had shown her _____ .

12. Booz told Ruth he would _____ her and made sure she had something to eat at _____ .

13. Booz eventually married Ruth, placing her in charge of his _____ , and their son was named _____ .

14. Booz also made a home for _____ .

15. _____ was the grandfather of David, the _____ , and from his family the _____ of the world would come.

Matching

Directions: In each blank, write the letter of the phrase that correctly identifies that person, group, place or thing. Each blank is worth 2 points. 20 possible points.

1. ___ Bethlehem

2. ___ Noemi

3. ___ Ruth

4. ___ Orpha

5. ___ Obed

6. ___ Booz

7. ___ Elimelech

8. ___ King David

9. ___ Moab

10. ___ the Savior, Jesus Christ

A) grandson of Obed
B) Noemi's daughter-in-law who returned to Moab
C) Noemi's husband
D) came from Obed's and David's family

E) place where Noemi was from
F) went with Ruth to Bethlehem
G) place where Ruth was from
H) Booz's son

I) relative of Elimelech
J) protected by Booz

BIBLE HISTORY — WORKBOOK

| Unit Four
Section I | **I. Saul, the First King
of the Israelites** | Text
Pages
173-193 |

Perfect Score: 100   Score: _____

Completion

Directions: Complete and make each statement true and accurate by writing one or more words on each blank line. Each blank is worth 1 point. 80 possible points.

1. Samuel tried to tell the people that _____ was their King, but

   they insisted on having a _____ king to lead them to victory over their enemies and unite them.

2. God told Samuel that _____ would be the first

   _____ of His people.

3. Saul lived in the city of _____ , and he went to consult

   Samuel about finding his father's lost _____ .

4. Samuel poured _____ on Saul's head and told him, "Behold,

   the Lord hath _____ thee to be the king of His people, and thou

   shalt _____ His people out of the hands of their enemies that are round about them."

5. Samuel gathered all the tribes together at _____ and told them they had to discover whom among them God had chosen to be king by

   casting _____ .

6. _____ was at home when the people discovered that he was to be the king.

7. Saul sent a portion of cut-up _____ to every tribe with a message that what had been done to the oxen would happen to whoever did not

   follow him and Samuel in war against the _____ .

8. Saul's first army saved the city of _____ .

9. Saul's reputation was as great after he defeated the _____

   as Gedeon's was after he had defeated the _____ .

10. Saul was formally anointed King of the Israelites at _____ .

11. Samuel ordered Saul not to start the war with the _____
    until after he came and offered sacrifice, but in his impatience, Saul offered
    sacrifice himself.

12. Samuel told Saul that because of his disobedience, the _____

    would pass from Saul's _____ .

13. After Saul's victory over the Amalecites, he spared their _____

    and took their best _____ and _____
    for himself.

14. Samuel said to Saul, "Doth the Lord desire _____ and victims,
    and not rather that the voice of the Lord should be obeyed? For

    _____ is better than _____ . . . .

    Therefore, as thou hast rejected the _____ of the Lord,
    the Lord hath also rejected thee from being king."

15. Samuel went to _____'s home in Bethlehem and called him
    and his sons to a sacrifice.

16. Samuel commanded that the _____ son,

    _____ , who was in the fields, be brought to him.

17. Samuel anointed David, and the _____ of the Lord came upon
    David from that day forward.

18. David played the _____ to cheer Saul in his royal palace, and

    being pleased, Saul made David his _____ .

19. The Philistine giant, _____ , who was over

    _____ feet tall, offered a challenge to the Israelites that
    none of the soldiers was brave enough to accept.

20. Saul offered his daughter in _____ to any soldier who would

    slay _____ .

21. While David was bringing food to his _____ , he decided to fight the giant.

22. David said to Saul, "I have killed a lion and a bear, and this _____ shall be as one of them. I will go and take away the _____ of the people."

23. David's only weapons when he went to meet the giant were a _____ and five smooth _____ .

24. In response to Goliath's taunting, David said, ". . . This day I will slay thee and take thy _____ from thee. The _____ shall know that there is a _____ in Israel."

25. After David's victory, the people cried out, "Saul has killed his _____ , but David has killed his _____ of _____ ."

26. David and Saul's son _____ became very close friends.

27. _____ became so jealous of David that he cast a spear at him to nail him against the wall.

28. Saul told David that if he brought proof of having killed a _____ Philistines, he could marry his daughter _____ .

29. David killed _____ men, but Saul had already given _____ in marriage to someone else, so he gave _____ to David, who was very pleased, because he loved her.

30. When Saul's soldiers waited outside David's house, Michol said to David, "Unless thou save thyself this night, _____ thou shalt _____ ."

31. Michol helped save David by putting a _____ on the bed, with a hairy _____ , covered with clothes, at its head.

32. Though David wandered from place to place with _____ hundred men, he came out of hiding whenever the _____ attacked the Israelites, and Saul's _____ grew with each of David's victories.

33. In the desert of _____, David called out to Saul: "My lord, the king," while holding the piece he had cut from the hem of Saul's garment. Saul then knew that David could have _____ him, and for a while he ceased to _____ David.

34. In the desert of _____, David took Saul's _____ and a cup of water.

35. After David spared Saul's life a second time, Saul said to him, "I have _____. Return, my son David, for I will no more do thee _____, for thou hast spared my life this day."

36. Saul went to consult a _____ at Endor and told her to "bring up" Samuel.

37. Samuel told Saul, "He will rend thy kingdom out of thy hand and give it to _____, because thou didst not _____ the voice of the Lord. The Lord will deliver _____ with thee into the hands of the Philistines. Tomorrow thou and thy sons shall be with _____."

38. After Saul died, the Philistines cut off his _____, put his armor in the temple of _____ and put his body, along with his sons' bodies, on the wall of _____.

39. The Israelites at Jabes Galaad came by night and took the bodies of Saul and his sons and buried them in the _____ near Jabes.

40. David wept for the deaths of Saul and Jonathan; about _____ he said, "As a mother loveth her only son, so did I love thee."

Matching

Directions: In each blank, write the letter of the phrase that correctly identifies that person, group, place or thing. Each blank is worth 2 points. 20 possible points.

1. ___ Isai

2. ___ Valley of Terebinth

3. ___ Michol

4. ___ Mount Gelboe

5. ___ Merob

6. ___ Abner

7. ___ Samuel

8. ___ Engaddi

9. ___ David

10. ___ Ramatha

A) Samuel's burial place
B) place where Saul died
C) harpist
D) on shore of the
   Dead Sea

E) David's father
F) older daughter
   of Saul
G) David's wife
H) Saul's general

I) David defeated
   Goliath
J) Judge during
   Saul's reign

BIBLE HISTORY — WORKBOOK

Unit Four
Section II

**II. The King from Whom
The Redeemer Descended**

Text
Pages
194-208

Perfect Score: 100   Score: _____

Completion

Directions: Complete and make each statement true and accurate by writing one or more words on each blank line. Each blank is worth 1 point. 80 possible points.

1. David went to _____ and ruled as the King of _____ for seven and a half years before the other tribes accepted his rule.

2. _____ tried to make Saul's son king; after the son was killed, David was anointed king over all the Israelites at _____ .

3. The _____ , who occupied Jerusalem, mocked the Israelites, saying the _____ and the _____ would keep David out of their city.

4. _____ was the first man to scale Jerusalem's walls.

5. Jerusalem became David's new _____ and was henceforth the City of _____ .

6. King Hiram of the Phoenician city _____ gave up his alliance with the _____ and sent David cedar wood from the _____ mountains.

7. David tried to bring the Ark from _____ , but on the way to Mount Sion, _____ touched the Ark and was struck dead.

8. No one was allowed to touch the Ark except the _____ .

9. Since David was afraid to continue on with the Ark, he left it at the house of a _____ , who kept it for _____ months and was blessed during that time.

10. David put aside his royal _____ while he danced before the Ark. The _____ carried the Ark to Jerusalem and put it in the _____ which David had built.

11. Absalom was determined to become King and prepared to lead a _____ against David.

12. Absalom had told David he wanted to go to _____ in order to fulfill a _____ and offer sacrifice.

13. After Absalom had taken possession of David's _____ in Jerusalem, _____ , who informed David of all that was happening, told David to leave the _____ .

14. David's and Absalom's armies fought in the land of _____ .

15. Absalom's _____ got stuck on a branch and he was left hanging there.

16. _____ thrust three lances into the _____ of Absalom.

17. David arranged for Bethsabee's husband, _____ , to be placed in the _____ line of battle and left there to be slain.

18. _____ told David a story about a rich man who killed a poor man's _____ and prepared a meal with it.

19. After David repented of his sin with Bethsabee, Nathan told him, "The Lord hath taken away thy _____ . Thou shalt not _____ , but the child that is born to thee shall surely _____ ."

20. The second son of David and Bethsabee was named _____ .

21. David stored up materials and provided the workmen for the great _____ which he had dreamed of building but which he was forbidden to build because it was God's will that _____ build it.

22. David offered sacrifices of _____ bullocks, _____ rams and _____ lambs, and then Solomon was publicly anointed.

23. It was King _____ who united the Israelites and made them into a great nation.

24. The _____ were David's most powerful enemies.

25. A change in the way of _____ had started during Saul's reign.

26. During Saul's reign, the Israelites started using the _____ spear to throw at their enemies and the bow and _____ arrow for distances.

27. Before Saul's reign, each tribe had a head that led a _____ army, but Saul provided a _____ army, to which David added a bodyguard of loyal warriors.

28. David's council was made up of _____ wise and brave men.

29. Six thousand _____ throughout the country represented King David as _____ officers and _____ .

30. David's _____ gave orders to the _____ of the tribes, who had them carried out.

31. Taxes were paid in _____ , which was kept in storehouses throughout the country.

32. David's officers cared for the vineyards, the _____ cellars, the _____ cellars and the _____ where sheep grazed.

33. The Levites were divided into groups to care for the _____ , guard the _____ for the Temple and to be in the _____ that chanted the _____ music.

34. The religious hymns that David composed for _____ days are known today as _____ , many of which are prophetical because they foretold the _____ and triumph of the Messias.

35. Psalm 22 was written during the days when _____ persecuted David.

36. Psalm 22: "The Lord ruleth me: and I shall want _____ . . . .

For though I should walk in the midst of the _____

of _____ , I will fear no evils, for Thou art with me."

37. Despite his sins, David was a great _____ and a

_____ , and he reigned for _____ years.

38. David is a model for _____ because he showed sincere

_____ for his sins.

39. The _____ of David was a figure of the

_____ of Heaven later established on earth by David's

greatest descendant, the _____ .

Matching

Directions: In each blank, write the letter of the phrase that correctly identifies that person, group, place or thing. Each blank is worth 2 points. 20 possible points.

1. ___ Joab
2. ___ Hebron
3. ___ Chusai
4. ___ Jerusalem
5. ___ Abinadab

6. ___ tribe of Juda
7. ___ Philistines
8. ___ Hiram
9. ___ Lebanon Mountains
10. ___ Nathan

A) put Chanaanites in their army
B) housed Ark in Cariathiarim
C) prophet
D) cedar wood for David's palace

E) restored David to his kingdom
F) King of Phoenicians
G) built on Mount Sinai
H) Absalom's birthplace

I) captain of David's army
J) told David of Absalom's death

Unit Four
Section III

III. The Israelites under King Solomon

Text
Pages
209-219

Perfect Score: 100   Score: _____

Completion

Directions: Complete and make each statement true and accurate by writing one or more words on each blank line. Each blank is worth 1 point. 80 possible points.

1. Solomon became king before he was _____ years old.

2. Solomon offered _____ victims at the Tabernacle in

   _____ .

3. Solomon asked for the gift of _____ , which God gave him along

   with _____ , _____ and power, and God

   promised him a long _____ , provided that Solomon obeyed
   Divine Law.

4. After Solomon ordered an attendant to cut the child in

   _____ , he knew that the true mother of the child was

   the one who said, "Give her the _____ and do not

   _____ it," rather than the one who said, "Let the child

   be neither _____ nor _____ , but

   _____ it."

5. Many of Solomon's words of wisdom are in the Book of _____

   and he is said to have written the Book of _____ .

6. The _____ of Saba tested Solomon's wisdom with difficult
   questions, after which she said, ". . . Blessed be the Lord thy

   _____ Whom thou hast _____ and Who

   hath set thee upon the _____ of Israel."

7. Solomon made an agreement with King Hiram to provide

   _____ and _____ for the Temple.

8. The _____ of the Temple started in Solomon's _____ year as king, and the Temple took more than _____ years to build.

9. The Temple followed the same general pattern as the _____ and faced the _____ , but the Temple was twice its size.

10. The outermost and lowest Court was for the _____ ; the next Court within, on a higher level, was the Court of the _____ ; and the innermost and highest Court was the Court of the _____ .

11. The Tabernacle's _____ was lined with richly carved cedar wood overlaid with gold, and inside it were the golden Altar of _____ , the Golden Table containing the Loaves of Showbread and the Golden Seven-branched _____ .

12. The only thing placed in the Holy of _____ was the _____ with adoring cherubim.

13. The priests and _____ brought the Ark to the Holy of Holies in the Temple on the Feast of _____ .

14. At the dedication of the Temple, 22,000 _____ and 120,000 _____ were offered in adoration to God, and after Solomon's prayer of thanks, _____ from Heaven came down to _____ the victims.

15. The Lord promised Solomon that He would _____ him and his people as long as they walked in His ways.

16. In building the Temple, the Israelites returned to the command of the law to worship God in _____ place.

17. Solomon's palace consisted of _____ units, one of which was called the "House of the _____ of _____ ," and the furniture in it was all of _____ .

18. The empire which David had built up extended from the _____

to _____ .

19. The _____ years of Solomon's reign were peaceful and

are called the _____ age of the Kingdom of

_____ .

20. The city of _____ was built to protect caravans coming from

the _____ .

21. Solomon's contact with King _____ taught him the value of

_____ .

22. Every three years, Solomon sent ships to Tharsis in Spain for

_____ and _____ .

23. The people were taxed by being required to supply Solomon with

_____ and _____ ; also, they paid a tax

on every article they bought which was for the support of Solomon's

_____ .

24. Solomon divided the country into _____ provinces and

no longer respected the previous division of the Israelites into

_____ .

25. Solomon neglected to worship the true _____ , the one

important means for keeping the people _____ to him, and

eventually his wisdom left him.

26. The two causes which broke up the Jewish (national) unity which David had

wanted were: the heavy _____ , which made the people hate

Solomon, and _____ , since he built temples to the false gods

of his _____ wives, thus destroying the religious unity of

the Jews.

27. Solomon had put Jeroboam in charge of the _____
of Jerusalem and collecting the tribute (taxes) from the tribes of

_____ , _____ and Manasses.

28. The prophet Ahias tore his cloak into _____ pieces and said to Jeroboam, ". . . thus saith the Lord God of Israel, 'Behold, I will rend the kingdom out of the hands of _____ and will give thee _____ tribes. But _____ tribe shall remain to him for the sake of my servant _____, because he hath forsaken Me and adored false _____ and hath not kept My Commandments as did David his father. . . .'"

29. _____ encouraged the people's discontent and tried to make himself popular with them, but then he fled to _____ because Solomon tried to _____ him.

30. Solomon was buried in _____.

Matching

Directions: In each blank, write the letter of the phrase that correctly identifies that person, group, place or thing. Each blank is worth 2 points. 20 possible points.

1. ___ Ahias
2. ___ over seven years
3. ___ Egypt
4. ___ Brazen Laver in Temple
5. ___ Gabaa

6. ___ King Hiram
7. ___ forty years
8. ___ India
9. ___ fourteen days
10. ___ Jeroboam

A) held about ten thousand gallons of water
B) Solomon's reign
C) where Solomon obtained ivory and gold

D) people feasted at the dedication of the Temple
E) leader of a rebellion
F) sent Solomon horses and chariots
G) prophet

H) length of time for building of Temple
I) where Tabernacle was before the Temple was built
J) furnished wood for the Temple

Unit Four
Section IV

**IV. The Division of
Solomon's Kingdom**

Text
Pages
220-226

Perfect Score: 100   Score: _____

Completion

Directions: Complete and make each statement true and accurate by writing one or more words on each blank line. Each blank is worth 2 points. 80 possible points.

1. Solomon's son Roboam went to _____ to be anointed king

   when he was _____ years old.

2. The representatives of the people refused to acknowledge Roboam as king unless

   he reduced _____ .

3. Solomon's _____ advised Roboam to reduce taxes.

4. Roboam's friends advised him to demand _____ taxes to live
   as his father had lived.

5. Roboam said to the representative of the people, "My father made your

   yoke_____ , but I will _____ to your yoke;

   my father beat you with _____ , but I will beat you with

   _____ ."

6. Roboam   fled   to   _____ ,   but   the   prophet

   _____ forbade him to raise up an army to fight the rebels.

7. The tribes of Juda and _____ were loyal to Roboam, forming

   the Kingdom of _____ .

8. The other ten tribes, whose king was Jeroboam and who were known as the

   Kingdom of _____ , were not allowed by Jeroboam to worship
   at the Temple.

9. The _____ allied themselves with Roboam after Jeroboam's
   kingdom fell into idolatry.

10. Jeroboam founded a state religion and built temples where the people would worship golden _____ .

11. In Jeroboam's new religion, any man who could provide a bullock and seven rams for sacrifice could be made a _____ ; many altars of _____ were erected throughout the kingdom.

12. Jeroboam's capital was _____ , which appealed to the _____ of the people since Abraham and Jacob had both lived there for a time and had built altars there.

13. Jeroboam later moved the capital to _____ .

14. A prophet from the kingdom of Juda told Jeroboam that a future king named _____ would burn the false priests on an altar.

15. The hand which Jeroboam used to point at the prophet _____ and the _____ was broken in two, with ashes scattered on the ground, fulfilling the prophet's prophecy.

16. Jeroboam's wife went to see Ahias because her son, _____ , was sick.

17. The prophet told the queen that because Jeroboam had made false _____ for the kingdom God had given him, his family would be _____ out of the land, his _____ would die when she re-entered the city, his kingdom, Israel, would be overthrown by the _____ and his people would be taken captive.

18. Roboam forgot Semeias' command and declared war on _____ .

19. For three years, Roboam was a God-fearing ruler and his people sacrificed on one _____ according to the law, but eventually he followed evil advice and set an example of _____ , which the people followed.

20. _____ , Pharao of Egypt, invaded the Kingdom of Juda, taking the treasures of the Temple and the palace.

21. The neighboring nations, Egypt, _____ and

_____ grew stronger while the Jewish nation was helplessly

divided.

22. With so many men having to take part in wars, the trades and

_____ suffered, which led to a shortage of food and a high

cost of living.

23. Roboam reigned for _____ years and was succeeded by

_____ , who drove Jeroboam back into his own territory.

24. King _____ destroyed the places where idols were worshipped

and maintained peace for _____ years.

Matching

Directions: In each blank, write the letter of the phrase that correctly identifies that person, group, place or thing. Each blank is worth 2 points. 20 possible points.

1. ___ Roboam

2. ___ Aduram

3. ___ Sichem

4. ___ Abia

5. ___ Semeias

6. ___ Sesac

7. ___ Silo

8. ___ Abiam

9. ___ Ahias

10. ___ Asa

A) where Israelites buried Joseph's bones

B) prophet who forbade Roboam to fight rebels

C) where Ahias lived

D) King of Juda for three years

E) son of Jeroboam

F) prophesied death of Jeroboam's son

G) Abiam's son

H) King of Juda for 17 years

I) stoned while trying to put down a revolt

J) Pharao of Egypt

BIBLE HISTORY — WORKBOOK

Unit Four
Section V

**V. Holy Servants of God—
Their Preaching and Miracles**

Text
Pages
227-246

Perfect Score: 100   Score: _____

Completion

Directions: Complete and make each statement true and accurate by writing one or more words on each blank line. Each blank is worth 1 point. 80 possible points.

1. When General _____ 's troops made him king, he moved the capital from Thersa to _____ , a hill he had bought northwest of Sichem.

2. King Achab built a temple to _____ and a grove to Astarte to please his wicked, idolatrous wife _____ .

3. Elias told the King that his son would be punished by a great _____ for three years.

4. At God's command, Elias went to the Brook Carith, where he was fed morning and evening by a _____ .

5. In Sarephta, Elias told a woman to make him a cake with her last meal and said, "The Lord God of Israel will not let thy portion of meal and oil grow _____ until it pleaseth Him to give _____ upon the face of the earth."

6. The Lord answered Elias' prayer and restored the woman's _____ back to life.

7. God told Elias in the third year of the drought, "Go, show thyself to Achab, that I may give _____ on the face of the earth."

8. When Achab had killed many of the true prophets, _____ , the governor of the King's household, hid _____ prophets in a cave and brought bread and water to them.

9. Elias told Achab to gather the Children of Israel before Mount _____ .

10. To prove who was the true God, Elias proposed a test to see whose God would put _____ under the wood for the sacrifices.

11. The 450 prophets of _____ called upon his name from morning to noon, but there was no answer.

12. Elias made sport of the false prophets' god by saying, ". . . perhaps he is _____ , or is on a _____ , or is asleep and must be awakened."

13. Before offering the sacrifice, Elias made a trench around the altar and poured _____ buckets of water over the bullock.

14. Elias said, "O Lord, God of Abraham, of Isaac, and of Israel, show this day that Thou art the God of _____ , and that I am Thy _____ . . . that these people may know that Thou art their God."

15. When the people saw the _____ of the Lord consume Elias' holocaust along with everything else, they fell on their faces and cried, "The Lord is _____ !"

16. Elias had to flee because Jezabel said _____ awaited him for killing her prophets.

17. After an _____ fed Elias a hearth cake and water, Elias walked for _____ days and nights to the mount of God, Mount _____ .

18. The Lord told Elias to return to Damascus, saying, "There thou shalt anoint Hazael king over _____ . And thou shalt anoint _____ king over Israel, and _____ thou shalt anoint to be prophet in thy place."

19. A prophet foretold that Acheb would die by a _____ death since he had spared the Syrian king who was "worthy of death for his

_____."

20. Jezabel paid two men to swear _____ against Naboth and kill

him because Achab wanted his _____ .

21. Elias told Achab that where dogs licked the _____ of Naboth, they would lick his blood also, that dogs would eat the flesh of

_____ , and that the Kingdom of _____ would pass from his house for causing Israel to sin against God.

22. Achab put on _____ , fasted and slept in sackcloth; God was pleased and He said He would not bring the evil in Achab's day but in his son's.

23. The prophet _____ was imprisoned for foretelling Achab and Josaphat's defeat.

24. Naboth's prophecy was fulfilled as Achab's _____ was being washed in the pool of Samaria.

25. Jehu killed _____ , became king of _____

and had _____ thrown out of a window.

26. When Achab was king of Israel, _____ was the wise and peaceful king of Juda, but the kings who succeeded both of them were weak and sinful.

27. Eliseus asked for the _____ of Elias, who promised to him,

"If thou _____ me when I am taken away, thou wilt receive what thou askest."

28. A fiery _____ and fiery _____ took Elias into Heaven by a whirlwind, and Eliseus took Elias' mantle and divided the

_____ as Elias had done.

29. Naaman obeyed Eliseus' command to bathe _____ times in

the Jordan, and he was cleansed from his _____ .

30. Eliseus retained the power to work _____ even after his death.

31. Job lived among the _____ , the descendants of Esau.

32. The Lord said to Satan regarding Job, "There is none like him in the earth. He

is a _____ and upright man. He feareth God and avoideth

_____ ."

33. After the Lord gave Satan power over Job's possessions, Satan took his animals, children and most of his servants, leaving Job to say, "The Lord

_____ , and the Lord hath _____ .

_____ be the name of the Lord."

34. Job told his friends, ". . . Even if God should kill me, I will

_____ in Him. I know that my _____
liveth and in the last day I shall rise out of the earth, and I shall be clothed

again with my _____ , and my flesh shall see my

_____ ."

35. God was pleased with Job, so He rewarded Job even in this life with new

health, with doubled wealth and with _____ sons and

_____ daughters.

36. God told Jonas to preach in the city of _____ , but Jonas was

afraid and entered a _____ headed somewhere else.

37. After the men cast _____ to see who was the cause of
the storm that was putting them in danger, and the lot fell upon Jonas, Jonas

told them to cast him into the _____ .

38. The Lord sent a great fish to swallow Jonas, where he remained in

its _____ for _____ days and

_____ nights.

39. The second time that God told Jonas to preach, he entered the city and cried out,

"Yet _____ days and _____ shall be
destroyed."

40. The men of Ninive believed Jonas to be from God, so they began a great

_____ ; all the people put on _____ and
did penance.

41. When God saw the humble hearts of the people of Ninive and their works of

penance, He had _____ and spared them.

42. Our Saviour foretold His _____ when He said, "As Jonas

was in the whale's belly for _____ days and

_____ nights, so shall the Son of Man be in the heart of

the earth _____ days and _____ nights."

Matching

Directions: In each blank, write the letter of the phrase that correctly identifies that person, group, place or thing. Each blank is worth 2 points. 20 possible points.

1. ___ Elias

2. ___ Naaman

3. ___ Thebni

4. ___ Mount Horeb

5. ___ Nineve

6. ___ Abdias

7. ___ Jezrahel

8. ___ Brook Cison

9. ___ Eliseus' servant

10. ___ Brook Carith

A) governor of Achab's household
B) great city of Assyrians
C) at the foot of Mount Carmel
D) became a leper after lying

E) where Elias was fed by a raven
F) the Thesbite
G) general of Syrian army
H) governed part of nation during Amri's reign

I) where Elias lived in a cave
J) city where Jezabel died

Unit Five Section I	**I. The Assyrian Invasions**	Text Pages 249-258

Perfect Score: 100   Score: _____

Completion

Directions: Complete and make each statement true and accurate by writing one or more words on each blank line. Each blank is worth 2 points. 80 possible points.

1. The kingdoms of Juda and Israel became wealthy, but the _____ were oppressed and were forced to labor hard for little pay.

2. The punishment of the kingdoms for their oppression of the poor and their other wickedness came first by a rebellion of the _____ and downtrodden, and then by the invasion of the _____ .

3. Israel's king tried to befriend the Assyrian king, but the king of Assyria besieged _____ , taking its inhabitants as captives and casting its king into prison.

4. The Samaritan, Tobias, who was one of the captives made to settle in _____ , never adored the golden calves but remained obedient to the law that commanded Jews to worship in _____ .

5. The king ordered Tobias to be put to _____ for burying the dead and giving help to their relatives.

6. When a new king was reigning, Tobias' _____ was returned to him.

7. The dirt from a _____'s nest blinded Tobias.

8. The older Tobias told his son, ". . . Do not turn away thy face from any _____ person. If thou have much, give _____. If thou have little, give the little _____, for alms deliver from sin and from death. Never allow _____ to reign in thy mind or in thy words."

9. Tobias told his son to find a faithful man for a companion and to go collect a _____.

10. Tobias' companion told him how to catch the fish and to cut out the heart, the gall and the _____.

11. The guide led the younger Tobias to one of his kinsman, whose daughter, _____, Tobias married.

12. The guide collected the debt from _____ and brought him to the wedding feast.

13. When the younger Tobias placed the fish's _____ on his father's eyes, his father recovered his sight.

14. The guide said, "The Lord sent me to you, for I am the Angel _____, one of the seven who stand before the Lord."

15. Before the older Tobias died, he foretold the fall of _____ and the rebuilding of Jerusalem after the Babylonian _____.

16. When Ezechias became king of Juda, he tore down all the altars that had been built outside _____.

17. Ezechias commanded the priests and _____ to purify the Temple, since false gods had been worshipped there.

18. After the _____-day purification of the Temple, Ezechias restored the services to the way they were during the time of _____ and urged people to pay the fruits and tithes ordered in the Law of Moses.

19. _____ told Ezechias that he was going to die.

20. The Lord heard Ezechias' prayer, so Isaias told him to go to the Temple on the third day and he would have _____ years added to his life; and the Lord promised to deliver his city from the hands of the _____ .

21. Contrary to the advice of Isaias, Ezechias formed an alliance with _____ and defied the Assyrians.

22. Ezechias prayed to God to deliver him from King _____ .

23. At night an Angel killed _____ men in the Assyrian camp, and the Assyrians returned to Assyria and left the Kingdom of Juda alone.

24. Under Manasses, the new King of Juda, Jerusalem was captured by the Assyrians and Manasses was taken captive to _____ .

25. When the Assyrians under Holofernes cut off the _____ supply to the city of Bethulia, its inhabitants decided to surrender if help did not come in _____ days.

26. Judith rebuked the chief men of Bethulia for setting a _____ to God's power.

27. Judith told _____ that she fled her city to escape the cruelty of the Assyrian _____ when it fell.

28. At the feast for the Assyrian officers, after Holofernes had become drunk and had fallen asleep, _____ cut off his head and hurried to _____ .

29. When the Jews attacked, the Assyrians found their leader dead; later, _____ was released.

Matching

Directions: In each blank, write the letter of the phrase that correctly identifies that person, group, place or thing. Each blank is worth 2 points. 20 possible points.

1. ___ Manasses

2. ___ Gabelus

3. ___ Sennacherib

4. ___ tried to kill younger Tobias

5. ___ Sara

6. ___ Holofernes

7. ___ Ezechias

8. ___ Tobias

9. ___ Judith

10. ___ Angel Raphael

A) giant fish
B) wicked king of Juda
C) Assyrian general
D) younger Tobias' companion

E) from the tribe Nephtali
F) widow
G) owed debt to Tobias

H) younger Tobias' wife
I) Assyrian king
J) God-fearing king of Juda

Unit Five
Section II

II. The Babylonian Captivity

Text
Pages
259-277

Perfect Score: 100

Score: _____

Completion

Directions: Complete and make each statement true and accurate by writing one or more words on each blank line. Each blank is worth 1 point. 80 possible points.

1. When Egypt and Babylonia were at war, Jeremias told King Joakim and the Jews to rely on _____ and not on an alliance with _____ .

2. The Babylonian king's son, Nabuchodonosor, captured the city of _____ and took the _____ from the Temple.

3. Joakim was made a subject of the king of _____ .

4. After Joakim rebelled against the Babylonians, Jerusalem was conquered, and Joakim's _____ was made king of Juda.

5. Nabuchodonosor burnt the _____ and took back with him to Babylon the king, seven thousand Jewish _____ and every skilled _____ .

6. Nabuchodonosor's vassal, _____ , was made the new king of Juda.

7. To remind the people of what would happen if they did not obey God and trust in God rather than in Egypt, Jeremias walked around wearing a _____ on his neck.

8. Sedecias joined with the Egyptians, so Nabuchodonosor laid siege to Jerusalem for the _____ time, during which time Sedecias had _____ imprisoned for preaching that all who joined with the _____ would be saved.

9. After the siege, most of Jerusalem was destroyed, including the beautiful _____ of Solomon.

10. _____ and some Levites rescued and hid the Ark of Covenant.

11. The sad sight of Jerusalem in ruins inspired Jeremias to write the _____ .

12. The Jews were forced to work hard to restore nearly all the Babylonian cities and to build the elevated terraces known as the _____ .

13. _____ , Ananias, Misael and _____ were Jews who were cared for and educated as members of the king's family.

14. _____ was a prophet who was one of the captives taken to Babylon but who was given great freedom.

15. When the elders threatened to accuse _____ of sin and condemn her to _____ if she would not sin, she said, ". . . But it is better for me to fall into your hands without doing it, than to _____ in the sight of the _____ ."

16. In answer to Susanna's prayer, the Lord inspired _____ to ask, "Are you so foolish that without examination of the _____ you condemn a daughter of _____ ?"

17. The first elder said he had seen Susanna under a _____ tree, but the other said he had seen her under a _____ tree, so it was clear that the elders were lying; they were put to death.

18. Nabuchodonosor had a dream that frightened him, but when he could not recall it, he called the _____ and the magicians to see who could tell it to him and explain it.

19. Daniel told Nabuchodonosor that his ability to tell him his dream came from _____ .

20. Since the king made Daniel _____ over the provinces of Babylon, the Jewish workers' _____ were lightened and they began to receive pay which they could use to buy their _____ .

21. The Jewish captives could not offer _____ , but they offered prayers and listened to the sacred writings in the _____ .

22. Daniel's three companions, _____ , _____ and _____ , did not go to offer sacrifice to the king's false god, though he had commanded it.

23. God sent an _____ to save the three young men from the fire, and they walked through the flames unharmed.

24. _____ delivered Daniel to the angry people, who cast him into a den of hungry _____ .

25. The prophet _____ was carried by an Angel to _____ to whom he gave boiled _____ and bread.

26. Daniel's _____ were eaten by lions.

27. King Baltassar and his guests drank from the sacred _____ which _____ had stolen from the Temple.

28. The writing on the wall at the king's banquet said, "_____ , _____ , _____ ."

29. _____ meant that the King was weighed in the balance, or judged, and was found wanting.

30. _____ meant that the Babylonian kingdom would be divided and given to the _____ and Persians.

31. The King had Daniel clothed in _____ , with a chain of _____ put about his neck, and he was made the _____ man in the kingdom since he was the only one who could explain the writing on the wall.

32. When the Babylonian army surrendered to the Persians, _____ became the next king.

33. Prophets not only foretold the future, they told the people what they needed to do to _____ God at the present time.

34. The four _____ prophets are those whose writings take up a large section of the Bible.

35. According to a tradition, the prophet _____ suffered martyrdom at the hands of a wicked king.

36. Isaias told the Jews to trust in God and not to fear their _____ , but to fear _____ .

37. The earthly king who would set the Jews free in Babylon was _____ , King of the _____ .

38. Isaias prophesied: "There shall come forth a rod out of the root of _____ , and a _____ shall rise up out of his root. And the spirit of the Lord shall rest upon him, the spirit of wisdom and of _____ , the spirit of counsel and of _____ , the spirit of knowledge and of _____ ..."

39. Isaias prophesied, "Behold, a _____ shall conceive and bring forth a Son, and His name shall be called Emmanuel."

40. Isaias foretold that the _____ of Christ would draw the people to herself, that all _____ would flow to His Church and that the _____ would be converted to God.

41. _____ wrote the Lamentations after the people of the kingdom of Juda were taken captive and Jerusalem and its Temple were destroyed.

42. Ezechiel prophesied in _____ , and from him we get the symbols of the four _____ .

43. _____ foretold to the day the time of the Jewish people's deliverance and the coming of the _____ .

Matching

Directions: In each blank, write the letter of the phrase that correctly identifies that person, group, place or thing. Each blank is worth 2 points. 20 possible points.

1. ___ St. John
2. ___ Nabuchodonosor
3. ___ Susanna
4. ___ Nathan
5. ___ St. Luke

6. ___ Baltassar
7. ___ Jeremias
8. ___ Evil-Merodach
9. ___ Daniel
10. ___ Babylon

A) usurper of the throne in Juda
B) prophesied between 630 and 580 B.C.
C) represented as an ox
D) prophesied between 600 and 540 B.C.

E) had his dream explained by Daniel
F) minor prophet in days of David
G) became a great center of Jewish learning

H) saved from death by Daniel
I) represented as an eagle
J) delivered Daniel to the people

Perfect Score: 100   Score: _____

Completion

Directions: Complete and make each statement true and accurate by writing one or more words on each blank line. Each blank is worth 2 points. 80 possible points.

1. Cyrus let the Jews return to Juda so there would be a friendly nation between

   himself and _____ .

2. Cyrus gave the Jews back the _____ and ordered that the Temple be rebuilt.

3. The Jews remained in Babylon as captives for _____ years.

4. The _____ and Babylonians had ruled over Juda while the Jews were in captivity.

5. _____ was the leader of the Jewish exiles who were returning to Juda.

6. As soon as the Jewish exiles returned to Jerusalem, they built an altar for the

   morning and evening _____ .

7. The Jews would not allow _____ , who said they adored the God of Israel together with other gods, to take part in building the Temple to the true God.

8. The prophets Aggeus and _____ encouraged the people to continue with the Temple building, and eventually King Darius I allowed them to finish it.

9. The Temple was completed after twenty years, in _____ B.C.

10. King Assuerus chose the Jewish woman _____ , to be his

    wife and her _____ , Mardochai, was given a position at the palace.

11. _____ ,   Assuerus'   chief   adviser,   hated

    _____ for defeating his plans to dethrone the king.

12. Assuerus ordered a general _____ of the Jews after believing

    Aman's lies that they were preparing a _____ .

13. When Mardochai commanded Esther to plead for the Jews, she told him to gather

    friends and fast with her for _____ days and nights.

14. Esther went before her husband the king and invited him and Aman to a

    _____ , even though the penalty for a subject going before the

    king without being called was _____ .

15. Aman built a _____ and intended to ask the king to condemn

    _____ to death.

16. Assuerus called in the _____ of his empire, who read to him

    the _____ of his reign.

17. The king wished to honor _____ for reporting the plot against
    his life.

18. _____ , thinking it was he who the king wished to honor, said

    that the man honored should be dressed in the king's _____
    and crown and set upon the king's horse and thus led through the capital streets.

19. At the second banquet, Esther asked for her people's lives to be spared and said,

    "_____ is our wicked enemy."

20. Aman was hung on the _____ which he had prepared for

    Mardochai, and the Jews were delivered from _____ .

21. _____ allowed Esdras and the Jews in Babylon to make a
    pilgrimage to Jerusalem and gave him a donation for the restoration of the

    _____ and ceremonies of the Temple.

22. In Jerusalem, Esdras ordered that all the _____ women be
    cast out of their homes.

23. Esdras made small copies of the Sacred _____ , bringing them
    back to the people.

24. _____ succeeded in having the walls of Jerusalem rebuilt in
    fifty-two days.

25. Each Jewish _____ was assigned a section of the walls to rebuild.

26. The Ammonite, _____ , lied to the king out of spite after Nehemias removed his goods from the Temple and put back the sacred

_____ , but the king found that Nehemias was loyal.

27. Nehemias refused to accept the gifts from the _____ , which were due to him as governor, and urged the rich to forgive their debts.

28. Manasses was banished from the city for marrying a pagan woman but was

appointed _____ by the king.

29. Manasses built a temple on Mount Garizim in Samaria, thus beginning the

_____ worship of the _____ .

Matching

Directions: In each blank, write the letter of the phrase that correctly identifies that person, group, place or thing. Each blank is worth 2 points. 20 possible points.

1. ___ Zorobabel
2. ___ Josue
3. ___ Manasses
4. ___ Esdras
5. ___ Assuerus

6. ___ Nehemias
7. ___ Cyrus
8. ___ Zacharias
9. ___ Mardochai
10. ___ Aman

A) tried to dethrone Assuerus
B) prophet who urged the Temple be rebuilt
C) cupbearer of Artaxerxes I

D) returned sacred vessels to the Jews
E) stood at gates of King Assuerus
F) belonged to family of the kings of Juda
G) son of Darius I

H) priest who restored religious worship in Palestine
I) high priest who accompanied Zorobabel
J) started a schism

BIBLE HISTORY — WORKBOOK

Unit Five
Section IV

IV. The Last Days of the Kingdom of Juda

Text
Pages
289-304

Perfect Score: 100   Score: _____

Completion

Directions: Complete and make each statement true and accurate by writing one or more words on each blank line. Each blank is worth 1 point. 80 possible points.

1. After the time of Nehemias, the _____ ruled eastern Asia.

2. In Juda, there were Jews who lived according to the commandments and Law of _____ , and there were also Jews who married pagan women and worshipped in _____ on Mount _____ .

3. Asia became _____ when Alexander defeated the _____ .

4. The Jewish people refused to pay tribute to _____ , so he marched against _____ .

5. Alexander had seen the high priest in a _____ , and he offered sacrifice.

6. Under Alexander, the Jews were allowed to worship God according to their _____ .

7. After Alexander's death, the empire was divided among his generals into _____ parts.

8. Simon, the _____ of the Temple, told Apollinius that the large amount of money in the Temple _____ was not needed for the _____ and could be turned over to the _____ .

9. Seleucus' officer Heliodorus insisted on taking the treasure in the Temple, although _____ told him that it either belonged to individuals or was set aside for the care of _____ and

_____ .

10. A heavenly _____ , clad in _____ armor and seated on a horse, accompanied by two beautiful, strong young men prevented Heliodorus from taking the money, and they

_____ him without mercy.

11. Onias offered a _____ for Heliodorus' health and

_____ .

12. The heavenly messengers told Heliodorus to thank _____ since it was because of him that God had spared his life.

13. When Antiochus _____ was king of _____ ,

he sold many Jews as _____ and killed others, plundered

the _____ of the Temple and offered _____ animals on the altar.

14. Antiochus turned the _____ into a place where pagans

adored their idols, and Jews were punished by _____ for observing the Sabbath and other Jewish laws.

15. Many Jews who were not sold into _____ fled, so Antiochus

had _____ from other countries take their place.

16. The persecutions made the Jews _____ , and their heroism

was so great that many even suffered _____ .

17. The ninety-year-old _____ refused to eat the flesh of

_____ and, for his obedience to God, was beaten to death.

18. The oldest of the Machabee brothers told the King, "We are ready to

_____ rather than to _____ the laws of

God which we received from our _____ ."

19. The mother of the seven Machabee brothers watched her sons be cruelly tortured and put to death, but she encouraged them to be brave and not to turn away from _____ .

20. The youngest Machabee said to the King, "Thou hast not yet escaped the _____ of God, Who _____ all things. My brothers, having undergone a short _____ , are now in _____ life . . ."

21. _____ and his _____ sons fled Jerusalem during Antiochus' persecution and led a group of men to drive the King's forces from the towns.

22. During the period of peace under the leadership of Judas _____ , the _____ was purified, and a new altar was _____ by offering victims on it for _____ days.

23. Judas defeated the _____ , _____ and the _____ and brought the Jewish _____ back to Jerusalem.

24. Some of Judas' soldiers had touched _____ from one of the heathen temples.

25. Judas sent money to Jerusalem and had _____ offered for the _____ of his soldiers, saying, "It is a holy and _____ thought to pray for the _____ , that they may be loosed from _____ ."

26. On his way to _____ , Antiochus' flesh fell from his bones and a terrible stench came from his body. God did not hear his prayer because his repentance was not _____ .

27. Antiochus _____ , who was king of Syria, tried to get Judas Machabeus to allow _____ to act as high priest.

28. _____ and _____ appeared to Judas in

a vision and promised him and his army of _____ men victory

against _____ and his 35,000 _____

soldiers.

29. Judas made an alliance with _____ but was slain shortly

afterwards while encamped at _____ .

30. Jonathon succeeded his brother Judas after a while, but was murdered and

succeeded by _____ .

31. The _____ were the only nation who worshipped the true God
at that time.

32. After the Machabees, the Jews engaged in _____ war. Then a

Roman emperor appointed _____ to be king of Juda, thus

fulfilling _____ 's prophecy regarding the passing of the

scepter from _____ and the _____ of the

Nations Who was about to come—that is, the _____ which
the world was awaiting.

Matching

Directions: In each blank, write the letter of the phrase that correctly identifies
that person, group, place or thing. Each blank is worth 2 points. 20 possible points.

1. ___ Simon

2. ___ Seleucus IV

3. ___ Nicanor

4. ___ Mount Sion

5. ___ Mathathias

6. ___ Mount Garizim

7. ___ Antiochus Epiphanes

8. ___ Onias

9. ___ Jeremias

10. ___ Alexander

A) father of Judas
   Machabeus
B) high priest
C) unfaithful Jews
   worshipping in
   Samaria
D) allowed Jews to
   worship God
E) jealous of Onias

F) defeated by Judas
   Machabeus at
   Bethoron
G) appeared with Onias
   to Machabeus in
   a vision
H) Syrians' fortress
   which Machabeus
   beseiged

I) sent Heliodorus to
   take the Temple
   treasure
J) forbade Jews to
   offer sacrifices to
   God

The
New Testament

| Unit Six Section I | **I. Preparation of the World for the Messias** | Text Pages 307-321 |

Perfect Score: 100   Score: _____

Completion

Directions: Complete and make each statement true and accurate by writing one or more words on each blank line. Each blank is worth 1 point. 80 possible points.

1. At the time of Our Lord's birth, the Promised Land, or Palestine, was about the size of the U.S. state of _____ .

2. Nazareth was one of the principal towns of _____ , one of the three provinces on the west of the River _____ .

3. Herod rebuilt the city of Samaria and gave it the name of _____ .

4. _____ was the last capital of the kings of the Ten Tribes.

5. Not many Jews lived in the country called _____ to the southeast of the Jordan during the time of Our Lord.

6. The neighborhood of the ten cities which the Romans built in the northeastern part of Palestine were known as _____ , and Palestine was a _____ province.

7. Herod was appointed King of Palestine by the Roman ruler, _____ ; the people hated Herod because he was not a _____ and because of his great _____ .

8. Herod's kingdom was divided among his sons: _____ , Herod _____ and Herod _____ .

9. _____ governed Judea and Samaria after Herod, but these were taken from him and given to a _____ , or governor, who only visited Jerusalem on great Jewish _____ .

10. The Romans sold the privilege of collecting taxes from the Jews to _____ who oppressed the people and were considered to be _____ if they were Jewish.

11. The coin that is called a "penny" in the Gospel was the _____ , worth _____ cents.

12. The "talent" in the Gospel was equivalent to about _____ dollars.*

13. Only _____ money could be offered in the Temple, so there were money changers there.

14. The Jewish people had changed their way of living very little from the time of _____ to the time of Our Lord.

15. The Jewish women wore a _____ on their heads, while the men wore wool wrapped in the style of a _____ .

16. Jewish houses were built mostly out of _____ , and they usually consisted of _____ room(s).

17. The custom when eating was to recline on _____ , and all ate with their _____ from a common dish.

18. The Jews washed their _____ before entering a house, sitting down at table or going to bed.

19. The people in Galilee lived by _____ and farming; the people in Judea mainly herded sheep and _____ and tilled the soil; and the people in Samaria mostly did _____ .

20. The third hour for the Jews was _____ a.m., and the twelfth hour was _____ p.m.

*Due to inflation, the current dollar amount of a talent, or of any Roman or Jewish coin used during Our Lord's time, is significantly larger than that given in BIBLE HISTORY, which was first published in 1931.

21. A lamb was sacrificed each morning and evening to acknowledge God's _____ of all things.

22. The two feasts added to the Jewish calendar since the time of Moses were the Feast of _____ commemorating Queen Esther's saving the Jews, and the Feast of the _____ honoring Judas Machabeus' dedication of the Altar and Temple.

23. The Jewish Sanhedrin was made up of seventy-one _____, elders and scribes and was presided over by a _____ .

24. The Sanhedrin had authority over all _____ matters and could pass a _____ on anyone who disobeyed the law, but the power to condemn someone to death was reserved to the Roman _____ .

25. Sacrifices were offered only in the _____ in Jerusalem, but the Jews met in _____ for religious instruction and Scripture reading.

26. When someone was "cast out of the synagogue" in the Bible, that means the person was _____ from the religious society of the Jews.

27. The men who instructed the people in the Law of Moses and translated the Scriptures were known as the _____ .

28. Though the Scribes belonged to various groups, most belonged to the party of the _____ .

29. The Pharisees' purpose was to preserve the Sacred Scriptures and keep them free from _____ .

30. The Pharisees became more interested in the _____ of the law than in its spirit.

31. Pharisees wore larger _____ , bands of parchment containing sacred texts, than other Jews.

32. The _____ did not believe in the resurrection of the _____ or in the life of the world to come.

33. Most of the Sanhedrin members belonged to the party of the _____ _____ , worldly men who mocked the Pharisees for their strictness but who followed the external observances of the law because they _____ the people.

34. The _____ lived in communities apart from the people like certain monks but carried their _____ to excess.

35. The _____ took a vow to serve God with great penance and _____ .

36. Galileans were not esteemed by the people of _____ because they were not as highly _____ and they spoke in a _____ .

37. The people of Samaria (Samaritans) insisted that their own temple on Mount _____ was the only temple of the true God, and they only accepted the five books of _____ for their Bible.

38. The people of _____ and _____ avoided the people of Samaria as much as possible.

39. The four languages used in Palestine during the time of Christ were _____ , which was used in every-day life; _____ , which men in high positions usually knew; ancient _____ , the language of the Sacred Books; and _____ .

40. Since _____ the Great rebuilt the great Temple in Jerusalem after it had been partially destroyed by fire, it was called _____ 's Temple.

41. The Temple's _____ Place was sixty feet long and the Holy of _____ was thirty feet long.

42. Jewish men entered the Court of the _____ of the Temple, and Jewish women entered the Court of the _____ .

43. The Court of the _____ , through an _____ , was used as a marketplace for the buying and selling of animals used for sacrifices.

44. The high tower in the southeast corner of the Temple wall was known as the _____ of the Temple.

Matching

Directions: In each blank, write the letter of the phrase that correctly identifies that person, group, place or thing. Each blank is worth 2 points. 20 possible points.

1. ___ Gabbatha

2. ___ Cana

3. ___ Jewish shekel

4. ___ Sichem

5. ___ Pharisees

6. ___ Arimathea

7. ___ Caesarea Palaestina

8. ___ didrachma

9. ___ Sadducees

10. ___ Scribes

A) in province of Galilee
B) first capital of the rebel kings
C) "doctors of the law"
D) some were courtiers called Herodians

E) square where the procurator met the Jews
F) worth eighty cents
G) worth forty cents
H) in province of Judea

I) headquarters of procurator
J) despised those who did not observe the law

II. The Redeemer among Men

Perfect Score: 100   **Score:** _____

Completion

Directions: Complete and make each statement true and accurate by writing one or more words on each blank line. Each blank is worth 1 point. 90 possible points.

1. The Angel _____ told Zachary that he and Elizabeth would have a son, who was to be named John.

2. Because of his disbelief, Zachary was unable to _____ until all the things the Angel had foretold were fulfilled.

3. The Virgin Mary said to the Angel, "Behold the _____ of the Lord; be it done to me according to thy word."

4. When Mary visited Elizabeth, her heart was so full of joy that she said a prayer of praise and thanksgiving, a Canticle that is now known as the

   _____ .

5. Mary prayed, "My soul doth _____ the Lord and my spirit hath rejoiced in God my Savior. . ."

6. After his son was born, Zachary was filled with the Holy Ghost and prayed the canticle known now as the Benedictus, in which he said of the infant John, "And

   thou, child, shalt be called the _____ of the Most High; for thou shalt go before the face of the Lord to prepare His ways . . ."

7. An angel told _____ that Mary would be the Mother of the Savior; the Angel said, "Thou shalt call His name Jesus. For He shall save His people from their sins." This fulfilled the prophecy of Isaias: "Behold a

   _____ shall be with child, and bring forth a son, and they shall

   call His name _____ , which means 'God with us.'"

8. Mary and Joseph had to go to Bethlehem for the _____ that the Emperor Augustus had ordered for taxation purposes.

9. The Virgin Mary wrapped our Infant Lord in swaddling clothes and laid Him in a

   _____ .

10. The Angel said to the shepherds, ". . . I bring you good tidings of great joy . . .

For this day is born to you a _____ , who is Christ the Lord, in the city of David. . ."

11. The multitude of Angels praised God before the shepherds, saying, "Glory to God

in the highest; and on earth peace to men of _____ ."

12. Eight days after Our Lord's birth, He was _____ and given the name Jesus.

13. In accordance with the law of Moses, the Infant Jesus was presented to the Lord in the Temple, and Mary and Joseph offered the sacrifice of the poor—two

_____ or two pigeons.

14. God had promised _____ that he would not die before seeing Christ.

15. Simeon prophesied to Mary, "Behold, this Child is set for the fall, and for the

_____ of many in Israel, and for a sign which shall be

contradicted. And thy own soul a _____ shall pierce, that out of many hearts thoughts may be revealed."

16. The widow and prophetess, _____ , knew when she saw the Infant Jesus that she had seen the Saviour of the world.

17. After Herod told the wise-men to go to Bethlehem, the _____ went before them again and stood over the place where Jesus was.

18. The wise-men brought the Christ Child gold, _____ and myrrh, and afterwards the Angel told them not to return to

_____ .

19. Herod ordered that every little boy who was _____ years old or younger, in Bethlehem and the country around it, be killed. This fulfilled the prophecy of Jeremias: "A voice in Rama was heard, lamentation and great

mourning; _____ bewailing her children, and would not be

_____ , because they are not."

20. An Angel had told Joseph to take the Child Jesus and Mary and flee into

_____ .

21. After Herod died, Joseph took Jesus and Mary back to their home at

_____ , in Galilee.

22. Every year Mary and Joseph went to Jerusalem to celebrate the great Feast of the

_____ .

23. In the year that Jesus was _____ years old, He went with them. He stayed in Jerusalem after the Feast, but His parents did not know it.

24. When Mary and Joseph finally found Jesus after three days, He was in the Temple

listening to the _____ and asking them questions.

25. Jesus asked Mary, "Did you not know that I must be about My

_____'s business?"

26. Our Lord lived in Nazareth, being obedient to Mary and Joseph for

_____ years, during which time _____ died.

27. Zachary's son John prepared for his great mission by living out in the desert,

wearing a rough garment of camel's hair and eating _____ and wild honey.

28. John preached near the River Jordan, saying, "Do _____ ; for the Kingdom of Heaven is at hand."

29. John fulfilled the prophet Isaias' words: "A voice of one crying in the

_____ : Prepare ye the way of the Lord; make

_____ His paths . . ."

30. People came to the Jordan, where John _____ them as a sign of their repentance and resolution to live a better life.

31. John said, "I baptize you with _____ . But there shall come One mightier than I, the latchet of Whose shoes I am not worthy to loose. He shall

baptize you with the Holy Ghost and with _____ ."

32. After Our Lord was baptized, the Holy Spirit in the form of a dove descended upon Him and a voice said, "This is My beloved Son, in Whom I am well

_____ . Hear ye Him."

33. After Our Lord had fasted for forty days and nights, Satan tried to tempt Him to

    turn the stones into _____ .

34. Our Lord told the devil, "Not in _____ alone doth man live, but
    in every word that proceedeth from the mouth of God."

35. Satan tempted Jesus to cast Himself off the pinnacle of the Temple and let the
    Angels catch Him, but Jesus quoted the Scripture: "Thou shalt not

    _____ the Lord thy God."

36. The devil promised to give Jesus all the _____ of the world
    and their glory if He would adore him, but Jesus answered, "The Lord thy God

    shalt thou adore, and Him only shalt thou _____ ."

37. When John saw Jesus again, he said, "Behold the _____
    of God, behold Him Who taketh away the sin of the world."

38. John and _____ were followers of John the Baptist who left
    John to follow after Jesus.

39. Our Lord told Simon that he would be called _____ , the
    Aramaic word for Peter, which means "rock."

40. After hearing of Jesus, Nathanael asked, "Can anything good come from

    _____ ?"

41. Our Lord called to the brothers Simon (Peter) and Andrew, "Come after Me, and I

    will make you _____ of men."

42. The publican _____ became one of Jesus' disciples.

43. Christ gave His disciples the power to heal, raise the dead, cure lepers and cast out

    _____ , and then He sent them out to preach the gospel.

44. John the Baptist was thrown into prison because he rebuked Herod Antipas for

    unlawfully marrying _____ .

45. Our Lord told John's disciples: "Go, and relate to John what you have heard and

    seen. The blind see, the lame walk, the _____ are cleansed. The

    deaf hear, the dead rise again, and the _____ have the gospel
    preached to them." Later, Jesus told the people, "There is not a greater

    _____ than John the Baptist."

46. Since Herod was pleased with _____ for dancing before him and his guests, he promised to give her whatever she wanted.

47. Herodias told Salome to ask for the head of _____ on a dish.

48. _____ , a member of the Sanhedrin, went at night to Jesus, who instructed him and told him that "unless a man be born again of water and the _____ , he cannot enter into the Kingdom of Heaven."

49. Mary Magdalen, filled with a spirit of repentance, bathed Jesus' feet with her _____ and wiped them with her hair.

50. Jesus taught the Pharisee named _____ that the person who is forgiven the most loves the most.

51. Our Lord told Mary Magdalen, "Thy faith hath made thee _____ ."

52. _____ was upset that Mary did not help her serve Our Lord.

53. Jesus said, "Mary hath chosen the _____ part, and it shall not be taken away from her."

54. When Our Lord sent out the seventy-two disciples, He said, "The harvest indeed is great, but the _____ are few. . . ."

55. Jesus' public life lasted for _____ years.

56. In the _____ in Nazareth, Jesus was asked to read to the people.

57. Jesus read from the book of _____ : "The _____ of the Lord is upon Me, wherefore He hath _____ Me to preach the Gospel to the poor . . ." Then Jesus showed the people how the Prophet's words referred to Himself.

58. Our Lord told the people, "A _____ is not held in honor in his own country."

59. The sermon in which Our Lord gave us the eight Beatitudes is known as the Sermon on the _____ .

60. Jesus said of Himself, "I am the way, the truth, and the _____ ."

61. Our Lord told His disciples, "When you are praying, _____ not much, as the heathens do. . . . your Father knoweth what is needful for you before you ask it . . ."

62. Jesus promised His disciples, "Ask and it shall be given you, seek and you shall find, _____ and it shall be opened to you."

63. Many people were attracted to Our Lord, Who in His kindness, said, "Come to Me, all ye that labor and are heavily burdened, and I will _____ you. Take up My yoke upon you and learn of Me, because I am meek and _____ of heart. . ."

64. At the wedding in Cana, _____ noticed the servants' distress over the wine and requested that Jesus help them.

65. The changing of water into wine was the first _____ that Our Lord worked in His public life.

66. The crowd murmured against Jesus for being the guest of the tax collector _____ , but Jesus said, "The Son of Man is come to seek and save that which was _____ ."

67. At _____'s well, the Samaritan woman was surprised that Jesus knew the secrets of her life.

68. It was unusual for _____ to mingle with the Samaritans.

69. Jesus told the Samaritan woman, "Whosoever drinketh of this water shall thirst again, but he that shall drink of water that I will give him shall not thirst forever. But the water that I will give him shall become in him a _____ of waters springing up unto life everlasting."

70. The Samaritan woman said to Our Lord, "I know that the _____ will come, and when He is come, He will tell us all things." Jesus answered, "I am He Who am _____ with thee."

71. When the Apostles brought food to Jesus, He told them that His meat was to do the _____ of Him Who sent Him.

72. When the Samaritan woman told people about Christ, they came to see for themselves, and then they acknowledged, "This is indeed the

_____ of the world."

Matching

Directions: In each blank, write the letter of the phrase that correctly identifies that person, group, place or thing. Each blank is worth 1 point. 10 possible points.

1. ___ *Nunc Dimittis*

2. ___ Nicodemus

3. ___ Ain-Karem

4. ___ Cana

5. ___ Emmanuel

6. ___ *Magnificat*

7. ___ Bethania

8. ___ *Benedictus*

9. ___ Andrew

10. ___ Old Testament priest

A) Zachary
B) Virgin Mary's Canticle
C) home of Mary, Martha and Lazarus

D) Zachary's Canticle
E) disciple of Jesus
F) Pharisee
G) home of Zachary and Elizabeth
H) wedding feast

I) Simeon's Canticle
J) God with us

How Christ Taught, Worked Miracles and Founded the Church

I. Christ, the Great Teacher

Perfect Score: 100

Score: _____

Completion

Directions: Complete and make each statement true and accurate by writing one or more words on each blank line. Each blank is worth 1 point. 90 possible points.

1. Jesus knew that though God did not create men for this world, many lived as

   though money, or _____ , or earthly power were the only things
   that mattered.

2. Jesus taught the people through _____ , stories which compared things of God to their everyday life.

3. To show people they needed to store treasures in Heaven and not on earth,

   Our Lord said, "Where thy treasure is, there is thy _____ also."

4. Our Lord taught that we should not worry about what we should eat or wear

   because the _____ neither sow nor reap and yet our Heavenly
   Father feeds them.

5. Jesus said, "Seek ye, therefore, first the _____ and His justice,
   and all these things shall be added unto you."

6. When Jesus told the crowd that whoever did His Father's Will was His brother,

   sister and _____ , He was teaching them that God loves those
   who do His Will and not simply those belonging to certain families or races.

7. To a disciple, Our Lord said, "No man putting his hand to the

   _____ and looking back is fit for the Kingdom of God."

8. "He that gathereth not with Me, _____ . No one can serve two masters," said Jesus, "for either he will hate the one and love the other, . . . You cannot serve God and _____ ."

9. In a story which Jesus told, "the beggar named _____ died and joined Abraham in Heaven, but the rich man who did not even give crumbs to the poor man was buried in _____ .

10. When the rich man in Jesus' story asked Abraham to send Lazarus to his five _____ who were still living, Abraham answered, "If they hear not _____ and the prophets, neither will they believe if one rise again from the dead."

11. The Pharisees performed the outward actions of the Law of _____ , but they did not have love for God in their hearts.

12. Our Lord told the people not to pray like the Pharisees, who prayed in public to be seen by others, but to pray to the Father in _____ .

13. Jesus said the Pharisees received their reward from _____ ; then He said, "But when you fast, anoint your head and wash your face, that you may not appear to men to fast, but to your Father Who is in _____ ."

14. In the parable of the publican and the Pharisee, the publican went back to his house justified because he had repented, saying, "O God, be merciful to me, a _____ ."

15. Jesus said, "Everyone that exalteth himself shall be _____ , and he that humbleth himself shall be _____ ."

16. God created the Sabbath to give people a day of _____ on which they could raise their hearts to Him; but the Pharisees taught that anything done on this day, including innocent enjoyment, was _____ .

17. Jesus showed people that the Sabbath was made for _____ , not _____ for the Sabbath.

18. The first person to go into the pool of _____ , after the Angel of the Lord moved the waters, was cured.

19. When the Pharisees persecuted Our Lord for curing the man at the pool on the Sabbath, He responded, "My Father worketh until now, and I _____ ."

20. Before curing the man with the withered hand, Jesus asked the Pharisees, "I ask you if it be lawful on the Sabbath Day to do good, or to do evil, to save _____ , or to destroy it?"

21. To show the Pharisees that they would not go to Heaven simply because they were the children (descendants) of _____ , Jesus told the story of a man who had made a great supper, but whose invited guests made excuses and did not come.

22. Jesus showed that only those who heeded the invitation of God to lead a _____ life would be allowed to enter Heaven, and not those simply belonging to a certain nation or tribe.

23. When God's chosen people did not heed His prophets, He sent His only-begotten _____ to call them to repentance, but they put Him to death.

24. Jesus foretold His own death in the parable of the Wicked _____ , who killed both their master's servants and his _____ .

25. Jesus explained that for punishment, the husbandmen (caretakers) would be destroyed and the _____ would be given to others.

26. With a whip, Jesus drove the money changers, merchants and animals out of the Court of the _____ and told the people, "Make not the House of My Father a house of _____ ."

27. Our Lord told the Pharisees that they had made the Temple into a den of _____ .

28. When Our Lord said, "Destroy this Temple and in three days I will raise it up," He was speaking of the Temple of His _____ .

29. Jesus did not destroy the Law of Moses; He _____ it to the people and helped them to obey it more perfectly.

30. Our Lord taught: "_____ your enemies, do good to them that hate you, bless them that curse you and _____ for them that calumniate you, that you may all be children of your Father Who is in Heaven."

31. Jesus said that even the _____ love those who love them, but that people should be _____ like their heavenly Father.

32. When Simon Peter asked the Saviour how often he should forgive those who offend him, he was told _____ times seven times.

33. To teach us that we should forgive one another from our hearts, Jesus told the story of a king who pardoned his servant's debt, but when the same servant was not merciful to another fellow servant, the king had the first servant delivered to the _____ .

34. Instead of taking an "eye for an eye" and a "tooth for a tooth," Our Lord taught that "If one strike thee on thy _____ cheek, turn to him also the _____ ," and if someone "take away thy coat, let him also have thy _____ ."

35. Our Lord said in the Sermon on the Mount, "Judge not, and you shall not be _____ ," and warned us not to try to take the mote out of our brother's eye when we have a _____ in our own.

36. The one sentence spoken by Jesus that sums up God's law of love is, "All things, therefore, whatsoever ye would that men should do to you, do you also to _____ , for this is the law and the prophets."

37. Jesus told the Pharisees that it was because of the _____ of men's hearts that Moses allowed divorce, but in the beginning there was no divorce. God made man male and female; and "what God hath joined together," said Our Lord, "let no man put _____ ."

38. To explain to the lawyer who his neighbor was, Jesus told the parable of the good _____ , who was the only person who showed mercy and was neighbor to the man who had been hurt by robbers.

39. When the storm caused the apostles to think their boat would sink, they awoke Jesus; He calmed the wind and sea and asked them, "Why are you fearful, O ye of little _____ ?"

40. Peter tried to walk to Jesus on the water, but his faith was not strong enough; Jesus, taking his hand, asked, "Why didst thou _____ ?"

41. Isaias wrote that the Messias would be called, "Wonderful, Counselor, God the Mighty, the _____ of the World to Come, the Prince of _____ ," and that He would "sit down upon the throne of _____ and upon his kingdom, to establish it, and strengthen it with judgment and with _____ from henceforth and forever."

42. Like the other Jews, the disciples thought the Messias would set up an earthly kingdom, bring back the scattered _____ , and form them into the greatest nation on earth.

43. Peter did not want Jesus to suffer and die as He had told His apostles He would; but, knowing that it was all part of God's plan, Our Lord said to Peter, "Go behind Me, Satan . . . thou savorest not the things that are of _____ , but the things that are of _____ ."

44. Teaching the people, Jesus said, "If any man will come after Me, let him _____ himself and take up his _____ and follow Me, for he that will save his life shall _____ it, and he that shall lose his life for My sake shall _____ it. For what doth it profit a man if he gain the world and suffer the loss of his own soul, or what exchange shall a man give for his _____ ?"

45. The _____ of James and John asked Jesus if her two sons could sit on each side of Him in His Kingdom.

46. Jesus told James and John they could drink of His _____ but that the privilege of sitting to His right or left belonged to those whom His Father chose.

47. To teach His Apostles humility, Our Lord told them that whoever wanted to be first, would have to be the _____ of the rest, because He Himself did not come to be ministered unto, but to _____ , "to give His life in redemption for many."

48. The _____ refused to give Jesus and His disciples a place to stay, so James and John wanted God to _____ them up.

49. The Son of Man did not come to _____ souls but to save.

50. Jesus did not want his disciples to forbid the man who was casting out devils in His name because, He explained, "He that is not against you, is _____ you."

51. The apostles scolded the mothers for bringing their children to Jesus when He was tired, but Jesus embraced and blessed the children and told the Apostles, "Unless you become as little _____ , you cannot _____ the Kingdom of Heaven."

52. Speaking to His disciples about children, Jesus told them, "He that shall _____ one of these little ones, it were better for him that a _____ should be hanged about his neck and that he should be drowned in the depths of the _____ . See that you despise not one of these little ones, for I say to you that their _____ in Heaven always see the face of My Father, Who is in Heaven."

53. Most of the apostles had been brought up to believe that the _____ would be an earthly king.

54. On the mountain with Peter, _____ and John, Our Lord's garments became white as _____ , His face shone like the _____ and He was entirely transfigured.

55. During Jesus' transfiguration, _____ and

_____ appeared with Him and spoke to Him about His death.

56. Peter cried to Jesus that they should make three _____,
but a cloud overshadowed them and a voice said, "This is My beloved

_____ in Whom I am well pleased. Hear ye Him."

57. When the apostles lifted their eyes, there was no one before them but Jesus,
Who told them not to reveal what they had seen until the Son of Man had

_____ from the dead.

Matching

Directions: In each blank, write the letter of the phrase that correctly identifies
that person, group, place or thing. Each blank is worth 1 point. 10 possible points.

1. ___ Pharisees

2. ___ Sabbath

3. ___ Lazarus

4. ___ Bethsaida

5. ___ Feast of the Pasch

6. ___ Moses and Elias

7. ___ James and John

8. ___ Mount Thabor

9. ___ Sichem

10. ___ Golden Rule

A) Sons of Thunder
B) exact in observing
   outward details
   of the law
C) when Jesus drove
   money changers
   from Temple

D) principal city of the
   Samaritans
E) summary of God's
   law of love
F) carried by Angels
   to Abraham

G) appeared with
   Jesus at His
   transfiguration
H) miraculous pool
I) day of rest
J) place of Jesus'
   transfiguration

Perfect Score: 100   Score: _____

Completion

Directions: Complete and make each statement true and accurate by writing one or more words on each blank line. Each blank is worth 1 point. 90 possible points.

1. Jesus grew up very poor; He was a _____ like Joseph.

2. Jesus lived in _____ , a town about which people used to joke.

3. In His public life, Jesus had no _____ of His own, but depended on the _____ of the people for His bodily needs.

4. Jesus said, "Blessed are the _____ , for theirs is the Kingdom of Heaven."

5. The poor in spirit are people whose hearts are not set on things of this _____ , whether they be really poor or rich.

6. People who are wealthy can still be poor in spirit if they use their riches not just for their own comfort, but for the _____ of God and the _____ of their fellow man.

7. When a rich young man asked Our Lord what he should do to have life everlasting, Jesus answered, "If thou wilt enter into life, keep the _____ ."

8. When the rich young man asked Jesus what else he needed to do, Jesus told him, "Go, sell whatsoever thou hast and give to the _____ , and thou shalt have treasure in Heaven. Then come and _____ Me."

9. After the rich young man showed that he did not have the courage to give up his riches, Our Lord said, "How hard it is for those that trust in _____ to enter into the Kingdom of Heaven. It is easier for a _____ to pass through the eye of a needle than for a rich man to enter the Kingdom of Heaven."

10. When the Apostles asked who, then, could be saved, Jesus said to them, "With men it is _____ ; but not with God. For all things are _____ with God," meaning that if a rich man does not trust in his riches but in God, and listens to His inspirations of grace, he can be saved.

11. Peter pointed out to the Lord that he and the other disciples had left everything for Him, so Jesus told them that they would sit on twelve thrones judging the twelve _____ of Israel.

12. Jesus said, "Every one that hath left house, or brethren, or sisters, or father, or mother, or wife, or children, or lands for My sake, shall receive a _____ in this life, and shall possess _____ ."

13. Though many rich people offered large sums to the treasury, Jesus said of the poor widow who put in a very small amount, "This poor widow hath cast in _____ than all the rest. For they did cast in of their _____ , but she of her _____ hath cast in all she had, even her last penny."

14. According to the Law of Moses, all Jews had to pay a tax of one didrachma known as the Price of the _____ .

15. Jesus had Peter pay the Temple tax, because He did not want to _____ others, even though He, as the Son of God, was not bound to pay it.

16. To warn people to beware of _____ , Our Lord told a parable about a man whose life was required of him by God after he had decided to hoard his goods, storing enough in a barn to last several years.

17. Jesus told a parable about a steward who cheated his employer to make _____ for himself to help him when he was forced to leave his job.

18. After telling the parable of the dishonest steward, Our Lord said, "Make unto you friends of the Mammon of iniquity, that when you shall fail, they may receive you into _____ dwellings."

19. The word Mammon means _____ ; iniquity, or _____ , is the means that many people use to acquire riches.

20. It is the duty of people who have money not to use it for selfish purposes, but to help others who are not so fortunate. Some ways of doing this are by providing medical care for the sick and by giving food and clothing and shelter to the _____ , the widow and the orphan.

21. When we share our wealth with those in need of help, those people will become our friends and will plead for us before the _____ of God.

22. Jesus said to His disciples, "By this shall men know that you are My disciples, that you _____ one another."

23. Our Lord often warned the Pharisees that love of their neighbor and the relief of God's poor, and not the mere _____ observance of the law, would open for them the gates of Heaven.

24. Jesus foretold the Great Judgment at the end of the world when the _____ would come with the Angels and gather the nations before Him.

25. Our Lord described how the shepherd would separate the _____ , who would be on His right hand, from the goats, who would be on his left hand.

26. At the Great Judgment, Our Lord will say to those on His right, "Come, ye _____ of My Father, possess you the Kingdom prepared for you . . . for I was hungry and you gave Me to eat; I was thirsty and you gave Me to drink; I was a _____ and you took Me in; naked, and you covered Me; sick, and you _____ Me; I was

in prison and you _____ to Me."

27. To the just, Our Lord will say, "Amen, I say to you, as long as you did it to one of these, My _____ brethren, you did it to _____ ."

28. The people who were not charitable on earth "shall go into everlasting _____ , but the just into life everlasting."

29. When Jesus was going to go to the centurion's house to heal his servant, the centurion said with great faith, "Lord, I am not _____ that thou shouldst enter under my roof. But only say the _____ and my servant shall be _____ ."

30. In Capharnaum, the crowd around Jesus was so large that four men let down a man with palsy through the _____ of the house that Jesus was in.

31. Jesus knew that some of the scribes thought He had blasphemed, so He cured the sick man, so they would know that He really did have the power to _____ sins.

32. The woman who suffered from blood loss touched the _____ of Our Lord's garment, causing Him to feel power go out from Him.

33. Jesus told the woman who touched Him, "Daughter, thy faith hath made thee _____ . Go thy way in peace."

34. Bartimeus and another blind man in Jerusalem called out to Jesus, "Son of _____ , have mercy on us."

35. When the people asked Jesus whether a certain blind man in Jersualem had sinned or whether his parents had sinned, causing God to punish him with blindness, He answered, "He hath been born blind that the _____ of God may be made _____ in him."

36. Jesus said to the people, "As long as I am in the world, I am the _____ of the world."

37. Our Lord put clay on the blind man's eyes and told him to wash in the Pool of

_____ .

38. Since Our Lord cured the blind man on the Sabbath Day, the Pharisees said of

Jesus: "This man is not of God, who keepeth not the _____ .

39. When Our Lord told the man whose eyes he had cured that He was the Son of God,

the man said, "I _____ , Lord," and then adored Him.

40. To cure a man who was deaf and dumb, Jesus put His fingers into the

man's _____ , and after spitting, He touched the man's

_____ and then said, "Ephpheta," or "Be thou opened."

41. The actions which Our Lord used to cure the deaf and dumb man were adopted by

the Church for use during the rite of _____ .

42. During the time of Christ, lepers could not enter cities or towns, they wore a veil
over their lips, and if someone came too close, by law they had to cry out,

"_____ , _____ !"

43. If a leper were cured, he would show himself to a _____ in
the Temple and purify himself according to the Law of Moses.

44. Of the _____ lepers Our Lord cured, only one came back to
thank Him.

45. When the cured Samaritan came back to Jesus, He asked, "Is there none found

to return and give _____ to God save [except] this stranger?"

46. Every human being, from Adam and Eve to the present day, has been forced to do
battle with the evil spirits who are constantly trying to lead us into

_____ .

47. When Jesus was teaching one day in the synagogue of Capharnaum, a man
possessed by the devil said, "Let us alone, Jesus of Nazareth. We know that Thou

art the _____ of God," but Jesus commanded the devil to leave
the man.

48. The devils in the possessed man at Gergesa answered Jesus, "My

name is _____ , for we are many."

49. The Gerasens wanted Jesus to leave them after he let the unclean spirits go into

the herd of _____ , who ran down a steep hillside into the sea and drowned.

50. When Our Lord told the man who had brought to Him his possessed son that all things were possible if he could believe, the man cried out, "I do believe; Lord,

help my _____ ."

51. The disciples wanted to know why they were unable to cast out the devil from the

boy. Jesus told them it was because of their _____ .

52. Jesus told His disciples, "If you had faith as a grain of _____ , you could say to this mountain, 'Move from here to there,' and it would move. . . .

You could say to this _____ tree, 'Be thou rooted up, be thou

transplanted into the sea,' and it would _____ you. This kind

of evil spirit is not cast out except by prayer and _____ ."

53. At first, Jesus did not cure the Gentile woman's possessed daughter. He said to her,

"It is not good to take the bread of the _____ and to cast it to

the _____ "; but the woman humbly persevered, and Jesus rewarded her for her faith.

54. The prophet Isaias wrote, referring to Jesus' miracles, "Say to the faint-hearted,

take _____ and fear not. God Himself will come and will save you. Then shall the eyes of the blind be opened . . . and the tongue of the dumb shall be free."

55. Our Lord proved His power over life and death when He brought back to life the man being carried in a funeral procession in the town of

_____ .

56. Even after word was brought that the daughter of _____

had already died, Jesus said, "The girl is not dead, but _____ ."

57. Taking the dead girl's hand, Jesus said to her, " _____ ," which means, "Little girl, I say to thee, arise."

58. Our Lord told Martha, "I am the _____ and the life. He that believeth in Me, although he be dead, shall _____ . And everyone that liveth and believeth in Me shall not die _____ ."

59. Lazarus had been buried _____ days before Jesus brought him back to life.

60. Caiphas told the Pharisees, "Neither do you consider that it is _____ for you that one man should _____ for the people, so that the whole nation may not _____ ."

61. Caiphas did not realize that by these words he had stated that Jesus was the _____ ; he did not realize that he had prophesied that Jesus would die for the nation.

62. The Pharisees tried to find something in Jesus' _____ that sounded like treason against the Law of Moses or against Roman authority.

63. _____ was living proof that Jesus was the Messias, so the Pharisees wanted him put to death also.

Matching

Directions: In each blank, write the letter of the phrase that correctly identifies that person, group, place or thing. Each blank is worth 1 point. 10 possible points.

1. ___ centurion

2. ___ Bethania

3. ___ Gerasens

4. ___ *Ephpheta*

5. ___ legion

6. ___ Price of the Soul

7. ___ Bartimeus

8. ___ stars fall from the sky

9. ___ *Talitha cumi*

10. ___ Naim

A) Temple tax
B) "Be thou opened."
C) blind man healed by Jesus
D) place where Lazarus lived

E) will take place when Christ comes again
F) said, "Lord, I am not worthy . . ."
G) where Jesus raised body to life in funeral procession

H) "Little girl, I say to thee, arise."
I) means "many"
J) wanted Jesus to leave their country

Perfect Score: 100   Score: _____

Completion

Directions: Complete and make each statement true and accurate by writing one or more words on each blank line. Each blank is worth 1 point. 90 possible points.

1. After Jesus' death and Resurrection, men have been able to see Him and hear Him

    and feel His presence in the _____ which He founded.

2. The _____ is the Kingdom of God on earth.

3. Though previously unable to catch any fish, _____ let

    down the _____ at Jesus' command, and it became so heavy
    with fishes that the boat almost sank.

4. Peter was ashamed of his sinfulness before Jesus, but Our Lord told him,

    "Fear not; follow Me and I will make you fishers of _____ ."

5. When Peter acknowledged that he and the disciples knew that Jesus was the
    Son of the Living God, Our Lord said to Peter, "Blessed art thou, Simon, son

    of John, because _____ and blood hath not revealed this to
    thee, but My Father Who is in Heaven. And I say to thee: thou art Peter, and

    upon this _____ I will build My _____ .
    And the gates of hell shall not prevail against it. And I will give to thee the

    _____ to the Kingdom of Heaven. And whatsoever thou shalt

    _____ upon earth, it shall be bound also in Heaven; and

    whatsoever thou shalt _____ on earth, it shall be loosed
    also in Heaven."

6. Our Lord's words showed that God would watch over Peter and protect him

    from _____ , and whatever Peter commanded would be the

    _____ of God.

7. Our Savior taught by means of _____ to help people understand what His Church would be like.

8. Jesus said that He is the true _____ , His Father is the _____ (vinedresser), and we are the branches.

9. "Every branch in Me that beareth not _____ , He will take away," Jesus explained; "and every one that beareth fruit, He will purge [prune] it, that it may bring forth more fruit . . . As the branch cannot bear fruit of _____ unless it abide in Me . . . He that abideth in Me and I in him, the same beareth much fruit. For without Me, you can do _____ ."

10. Jesus compared His Church to a sheepfold and Himself to a _____ .

11. Our Lord said, "I am come that they may have _____ and may have it more abundantly."

12. Our Lord taught, "I am the good _____ . I know Mine and Mine know Me, as the Father knoweth Me and I know the Father, and I lay down My _____ for My sheep . . . and there shall be one _____ and one shepherd."

13. But the _____ , whose own the sheep are not, flees when he sees the wolf coming.

14. In the parable of the cockle (weeds) in the field, the person who sowed the good seed is the _____ , the person who sowed the cockle is the _____ , the harvest is the end of the world, and the reapers are the _____ .

15. At the end of the world, the men who work iniquity will be cast into the furnace of _____ , where there will be weeping and _____ of teeth.

16. The Church can be compared to a net cast into the sea that gathers up fishes. When it is full, the fishermen pick out the good ones, just as the Angels will separate the _____ from the _____ .

17. The Church can also be compared to a grain of _____ seed, which is the least of all seeds, but when sown, it shoots out with great branches.

18. The Kingdom of Heaven is like a treasure hidden in a _____ for which a man sold all he had so that he could buy it, and it is like a

_____ of great price for which a merchant sold all he had so that he could buy it.

19. Our Lord made these comparisons to show us how we must be ready to make every

_____ in order to possess the Kingdom of Heaven.

20. A man cannot enter Heaven just because he belongs to the

_____ ; he must lead a _____ life.

21. To show how our good and bad works are like good and bad fruits, Our Lord gave

us the parable of the barren _____ tree; if it did not yield fruit, the caretaker would cut it down.

22. The members of Christ's Church do not receive the same

_____ ; the parable of the talents shows us that we must use them for Our Lord.

23. In the parable of the talents, the servant who received _____ talent dug a hole in the earth and hid his lord's money.

24. To the servants who doubled the talents entrusted to them, their lord said,

"Well done, good and _____ servant. Because thou hast been

_____ over a few things, I will place thee over many. Enter

thou into the _____ of thy lord."

25. To the servant who hid the talent entrusted to him, the lord said, "Take the talent

away from him and give it to him that hath _____ talents.

For to every one that hath shall be _____ , that he shall abound. But from him that hath not, that also which he seemeth to have shall

be _____ ."

26. In the parable of the sower, the _____ is the word of God. The seed that fell upon rocks represents people who hear and receive the word with joy, but who, having no roots, fall away in time of _____ . The seed that fell among the thorns represents people who yield no fruit because they are choked with the cares and _____ and pleasures of this life. The seed that fell on good ground represents people who hear God's word with a good heart and keep it and bring forth fruit in _____ .

27. Since death can come at any time, people must be ready at all times to give an account of themselves to _____ , their Judge.

28. Death may come at any time, like a _____ at night.

29. Our Lord said, "If a householder knew at what _____ the thief would come, he would not allow his house to be broken into. Be you also ready, for at what _____ you know not, the Son of Man will come."

30. Our Lord compared the Kingdom of Heaven to ten virgins, five of whom were wise, but five of whom were _____ and did not bring enough _____ for their lamps. The _____ they had been awaiting would not let them in to the marriage when they returned.

31. Our Lord said, "Watch ye, therefore, because you know not the _____ nor the hour."

32. In the Book of Wisdom there is a sentence which expresses beautifully the great love of the _____ for men: "My _____ are to be with the children of men."

33. After Jesus' ascension into Heaven, God's children would be united with Him by being members of the _____ , as the branches are united with the vine or as different parts of the body are joined to the _____ .

34. By showing men how to be good, Our Lord could make them _____ . By keeping them close to God, He could give them a foretaste of the joys of _____ .

35. To unite Himself with each soul, Christ instituted the Blessed _____ .

36. Trying to find a place to rest, Jesus and the Apostles went into the wilderness but they were soon surrounded by _____ thousand people.

37. Andrew told Jesus that among the crowd was a boy with five barley _____ and two _____ .

38. After the Apostles distributed the food, they gathered the fragments left into _____ baskets.

39. Jesus fled to a mountain because He knew the people wanted to take Him and make Him _____ .

40. When the people found Jesus in the synagogue, He told them, "You seek Me, not because you have seen miracles, but because you did eat of the _____ and were filled. Labor not for the meat which _____ , but for that which endureth unto life _____ ."

41. The people wanted to know what they should do, so Jesus said, "This is the work of God, that you _____ in Him Whom He hath sent."

42. Jesus said, "I am the Bread of _____ . Your fathers did eat manna in the desert and are _____ . . . I am the _____ Bread which came down from Heaven. If any man eat this bread, he shall live forever. And the bread I will give is My _____ for the _____ of the world."

43. To emphasize the importance of the Eucharist, Our Lord said, "Except you eat the _____ of the Son of Man and drink His _____ , you shall not have life in you. He that eateth My flesh and drinketh My Blood hath life everlasting and I will _____ him on the last day. . . . He that eateth this bread shall live _____ ."

44. The disciples were troubled at Our Lord's words; many of them said, "This saying is _____ , and who can hear it?"

45. Jesus told his disciples that His words are _____ and life.

46. "Remember," said Jesus, "I told you that no man can come to Me unless it be given him by My _____ ."

47. Our Lord asked the twelve apostles if they would leave Him, as many of the disciples had, but _____ answered, "Lord, to whom shall we go? Thou hast the words of _____ life. And we have believed and have known that Thou art the _____ , the Son of God."

Matching

Directions: In each blank, write the letter of the phrase that correctly identifies that person, group, place or thing. Each blank is worth 1 point. 10 possible points.

1. ___ the harvest

2. ___ Jesus' Church

3. ___ the five foolish virgins

4. ___ Peter

5. ___ good ground on which the seed falls

6. ___ cockle

7. ___ the five wise virgins

8. ___ Son of Man

9. ___ thorns

10. ___ good fruits

A) people who keep the word of God
B) went in to the marriage with bridegroom
C) the children of the wicked one
D) good works
E) the end of the world
F) sows good seed
G) riches and earthly pleasures
H) went to buy oil for their lamps
I) received keys to Kingdom of Heaven
J) like a net that gathers fishes

How Christ Redeemed the World and Returned to Heaven

Unit Eight Section I	**I. Christ, the Savior of Mankind**	Text Pages 461-467

Perfect Score: 100   Score: _____

Completion

Directions: Complete and make each statement true and accurate by writing one or more words on each blank line. Each blank is worth 2 points. 80 possible points.

1. Like the _____ lamb was slain so that its blood, being sprinkled on the doorposts, would save the Israelites' first-born from death in

   Egypt, the blood of Jesus saves from the death of _____ those who believe in Him.

2. The _____ of the Old Law could not open the gates of Heaven,

   but Christ, since He is God, paid the _____ that man owed to God by the sacrifice of Himself on the Cross.

3. Our Savior bought for man the right to enter the _____ .

4. The thirty-ninth Psalm talks about Jesus' coming to redeem us when it says,

   "Sacrifice and oblation Thou wouldst not, but a _____ Thou hast fitted to Me. Holocaust for sin did not please Thee. Then said I,

   behold I _____ . In the head of the book it is written of Me

   that I should do Thy _____ , O God."

5. The Pharisees criticized Our Lord for associating with known

   _____ .

6. So that people would understand that He came to save what was lost, Jesus asked what man would not leave his _____ sheep in the desert to find one that was lost, and then rejoice with friends and neighbors after having found it.

7. Our Lord said, "I say to you that even so there shall be joy in Heaven upon one sinner that doth _____ , more than upon ninety-nine just who need not _____ ."

8. To further illustrate His point, He asked what woman, having ten _____ , would not light a candle and sweep the house to find one that was missing and then rejoice with her friends and neighbors after finding the one she had lost.

9. Jesus said, "There shall be joy before the _____ of God, upon one sinner doing _____ ."

10. In the parable of the prodigal son, when the son who had wasted his substance away had come to his senses, he said to his father, "I have sinned against _____ and before thee. I am not worthy to be called thy son. Make me as one of thy hired _____ ."

11. The elder son was angry that his father had killed the fatted _____ and was having a party because of the younger brother's return, since he himself had never transgressed his father's _____ and yet his father had never done as much for him.

12. The father said to the elder son, "Son, thou art always _____ me, and all I have is _____ . But it was fit that we should make merry and be glad, for this thy brother was _____ , and is come to _____ again; he was _____ , and is _____ ."

13. So that people would know that it is never too late to return to Him, Jesus told a parable about a _____ who hired laborers early in the morning to work in his vineyard for a _____ a day.

14. In the parable of the laborers, the owner of the vineyard hired more laborers at the third hour, telling them, "Go you also into my vineyard and I will give you what shall be _____."

15. The vineyard owner hired even more laborers at the sixth, ninth and _____ hours; and in the evening he paid them, beginning with those that were hired last.

16. Those that were hired last received a _____ for their work, so those that were hired first complained when they were paid the same amount.*

17. The owner of the vineyard said to one of the first laborers, "Son, I do thee no _____ . Didst thou not agree with me for a _____ ? Take what is thine and go thy way. I will also give to this _____ even as to thee."

18. The Pharisees tried to entrap Jesus by bringing Him a woman who had been taken in _____ and asking Him what to do with her, since the Law of Moses commanded such a sinner to be _____ to death.

19. Jesus began to _____ with His fingers on the ground and said, "He that is without _____ among you, let him cast the first _____ at her."

20. After the Pharisees had left, the woman saw that no one remained to condemn her. Our merciful Lord told her, "Neither will I _____ thee. Go now, and _____ no more."

*Note: See p. 108 of this Workbook for some idea of the value of this coin.

Matching

Directions: In each blank, write the letter of the phrase that correctly identifies that person, group, place or thing. Each blank is worth 2 points. 20 possible points.

1. ___ the prodigal son

2. ___ Mary Magdalen

3. ___ "Go you also into my vineyard."

4. ___ "Behold the Lamb of God."

5. ___ Pharisees

6. ___ "Holocaust for sin did not please Thee."

7. ___ "Thou hast never given me a kid . . ."

8. ___ "Go now, and sin no more."

9. ___ adultery

10. ___ "He was lost, and is found."

A) householder
B) said by brother of prodigal son
C) were scandalized by Jesus
D) punishable by stoning under Law of Moses

E) said by father of prodigal son
F) said by Jesus to a sinful woman
G) kissed Jesus' feet
H) said by John the Baptist

I) fed the swine during a famine
J) thirty-ninth Psalm

Unit Eight
Section II

II. The Passion and Death of Christ

Text
Pages
468-525

Unit Eight
Section II
Subheadings 1 and 2

1. The Enemies of Christ Plot against Him
2. Christ Institutes the Holy Eucharist

Text
Pages
468-497

Perfect Score: 100   Score: _____

Completion

Directions: Complete and make each statement true and accurate by writing one or more words on each blank line. Each blank is worth 1 point. 90 possible points.

1. Our Lord spent the last six months of his life in and about

   _____ .

2. At the time before Our Lord's Passion, the _____ of some had begun to weaken, since they had expected the Messias to be an earthly leader who would free them from Roman power.

3. The love that some had for Jesus had been selfish, since they only followed after Him because they thought He would bring them earthly

   _____ , and their love eventually turned to hatred.

4. The worst sin against the Law of Moses was _____ , since it is a direct insult to God.

5. When Jesus spoke of God as His Father, the Pharisees said that He was

   _____ .

6. Our Lord told the people that if they did not believe His word, they should believe

   His _____ .

7. Jesus said, "He that is of God _____ the words of God."

8. To the Pharisees, Our Lord said, "I seek not My own _____ . There is One that seeketh and judgeth. Amen, amen, I say to you, if any man

   keep My word, he shall not see _____ forever."

9. When the Pharisees challenged Our Lord on His statements, He said, "Abraham, your father, rejoiced that he might see My _____. He saw it and was glad."

10. The Pharisees asked Jesus angrily how He could have seen Abraham. Jesus answered, "Amen, amen, I say to you, before Abraham was made, _____."

11. Jesus had made Himself equal to God by speaking the same words that God had spoken to _____ from the burning bush.

12. Herod thought Jesus might be _____ returned from the dead.

13. When the chief priests and Pharisees asked their agents why they had not brought Our Lord to them, the agents answered, "Never did a man _____ like this man." The Pharisees responded, " . . . It is only the _____ people, who know not the law, that follow after him."

14. Nicodemus, a secret follower of Jesus, rebuked the Pharisees, saying, "Doth our law judge any man unless it first _____ him and know what he doth?"

15. Martha's sister, _____ , poured valuable ointment on Jesus' head, and after anointing His feet, she wiped them with her hair.

16. Judas Iscariot spoke up and said that the ointment should have been sold so that the money could have been given to the _____ .

17. Our Lord told Judas, ". . . For the _____ you have always with you . . . But Me you have not always. She is come beforehand to anoint My body for the _____ ."

18. Our Lord instructed two apostles to go to a town and bring back the _____ of an ass, telling them what to answer if anyone questioned them.

19. These things were done in order to fulfill the prophecy of Isaias: "Behold thy _____ cometh to thee, _____ and sitting upon an ass."

20. At the sight of Jesus riding upon the ass, the crowds spread their cloaks on

the ground, and holding the branches of _____ trees, they

shouted, "Hosanna to the Son of David! _____ is He that
cometh in the name of the Lord! Hosanna in the highest!"

21. Some of the Pharisees wanted Our Lord to rebuke His disciples, but He replied

that if His followers said nothing, the _____ would cry out.

22. Jesus said, "Jerusalem, Jerusalem, thou that killest the prophets and stonest
them that are sent unto thee, how often would I have gathered together

thy _____ as a hen doth gather her _____
under her wing, and thou wouldst not."

23. Weeping over Jerusalem, Jesus said, "For the days shall come upon thee, and

thine_____ shall cast a trench about thee, and compass
thee around and straiten thee on every side, and beat thee flat to the ground, and
thy children who are in thee; and they shall not leave in thee a stone upon

a _____ , because thou hast not known the time of
thy salvation."

24. To the Pharisees who were angry that even the children praised Jesus, He

answered, "Have you never read, 'Out of the mouths of _____
hath come forth praise'?"

25. Some curious _____ asked Philip if they could see Jesus.

26. After the Saviour's death, the apostles preached the Gospel to all people,

regardless of _____ or color, and all peoples would give glory to
Christ the King.

27. Our Lord said, ". . . unless the grain of wheat, falling into the ground, die, it

remaineth alone. But if it die, it bringeth forth much _____ .

He that loveth his life shall _____ it; he that hateth his life

in this world, _____ it unto life eternal."

28. Our Lord prayed, "Father, glorify Thy _____ "; a voice from
Heaven answered, "I have both glorified it, and I will glorify it

_____ ."

29. Jesus told the people, "This voice came, not because of Me, but for your sake. Now has judgment come upon the world. Now shall the _____ of this world be cast out. But I, when I am lifted up from earth, will draw all things to _____ ."

30. When Peter remarked that the fig tree which Jesus cursed had withered, Jesus said, "Amen, I say to you, if you shall have faith, and waver not . . . if you shall say to this _____ , 'Take up thyself and cast thyself into the sea,' it shall be done."

31. Our Lord said He would tell the Pharisees by what _____ He did these things if they would answer whether the _____ of John was from Heaven or from men, but they would not answer.

32. Hoping to be able to accuse Him of treason, the enemies of Our Lord sent spies to ask Him if it were lawful to pay tribute to the Roman _____ .

33. Pointing out that Caesar's image was imprinted on a coin, Jesus answered, "Render, therefore, to Caesar the things that are Caesar's; and to _____ , the things that are _____ 's."

34. Jesus challenged the Pharisees by asking them how David was able to call Christ his Lord if Christ was the _____ of David.

35. Satan entered into the heart of _____ .

36. The chief priests offered _____ pieces of silver to Jesus' betrayer.

37. On the first of the seven days of the Feast of the Passover, in which the Jews celebrated the anniversary of their deliverance from the Egyptians, they ate the _____ lamb.

38. Before Jesus ate the Paschal supper with His disciples, He told them, "With _____ have I desired to eat this Pasch with you before I suffer."

39. Our Lord passed the chalice to His apostles and said, "I will no more drink of the fruit of the _____ until that day when I shall drink it with you in the Kingdom of My Father."

BIBLE HISTORY — WORKBOOK

40. To stop the apostles' argument, Jesus said, "For which is greater, he that sitteth at table or he that serveth? Is it not he that sitteth at table? But I am in the midst of you, as he that _____ ."

41. When Jesus told Peter he could not have any part with Him if he did not allow Jesus to wash him, Peter said, "Lord, not only my _____ , but also my hands and head."

42. Teaching His disciples to serve each other, Our Lord said, "For I have given you an example, that as I have done to you, so do you also. The servant is not greater than his _____ ; neither is the apostle greater than He that sent him."

43. Jesus told the apostles that one of them would betray Him and said, "Woe to that man by whom the Son of Man shall be betrayed. It were better for him had he never been _____ ."

44. _____ rested his head upon Jesus' bosom.

45. Referring to His betrayer, Our Lord said, "He it is to whom I reach bread _____ ," and He handed Judas the bread, saying, "That which thou dost, do _____ ."

46. Jesus gave thanks to God, blessed the unleavened bread, broke it and gave it to His apostles, saying, "Take ye and eat. This is My _____ ."

47. Our Lord took the chalice filled with wine, and, giving thanks, He passed it to them, saying, "Drink ye all of this. For this is My _____ of the New Testament, which shall be shed for many, unto remission of _____ ."

48. After Our Lord instituted the Holy Eucharist, He said to His apostles, "Do this as often as you shall do it, for the _____ of Me," thus giving to them and their successors, the priests of the Catholic Church, the power to change bread and wine into His Body and _____ .

49. By the institution of the Eucharist, the prophecy of Malachias was fulfilled: "From the rising of the sun even to the going down, My name is great among the Gentiles. And in every place there is _____, and there is offered to My name a clean _____. For My name is great among the Gentiles, saith the Lord of Hosts."

50. The new commandment Our Lord gave to His disciples was: "That you love one another, as I have loved you, that you also love one another. By this shall all men know that you are My _____ ..."

51. Our Lord foretold that the disciples would be scandalized in Him as it is written in the Scriptures, "I will _____ the shepherd, and the sheep of the flock will be dispersed."

52. Our Lord told Peter, "I have prayed for thee, that thy faith fail not; and thou being once converted, _____ thy brethren."

53. Our Lord foretold that _____ would deny Him three times before the cock crowed.

54. Our Lord comforted His disciples, saying, "In My Father's house there are many _____; I go to prepare a place for you. I will come again, and will take you to Myself, that where I am, you also may be."

55. Thomas did not understand the Savior's words, so Jesus said, "I am the way, and the _____, and the life. No man cometh to the Father, but by Me."

56. Our Lord told _____ that He is in the Father and the Father is in Him.

57. Our Lord told the apostles that if they loved Him, they would keep His _____; and He would ask the Father to send them the _____ of truth, Who would abide with them forever and would be in them.

58. Jesus said, "I will not leave you _____; I will come to you."

59. The Holy Ghost that the Father would send would _____ the disciples all things and bring to their minds whatsoever Jesus had taught them.

60. On the way to the Mount of Olives, Our Lord taught the apostles, "You are my _____ if you do the things that I command you. . . . And whatsoever you shall ask of the Father in My _____, He will give it to you."

61. Jesus prayed to the Father: "Father, the _____ is come; glorify Thy Son, that Thy Son may glorify _____."

62. In the Garden of Gethsemani, Our Lord told His apostles, "My soul is sorrowful even unto _____."

63. Our Lord prayed, saying, "My Father, if it be possible, let this _____ pass from Me. Nevertheless, not as I will, but as Thou wilt." An angel strengthened Jesus in His agony, and His sweat became as drops of _____.

64. The first time that Jesus found Peter and the other two apostles sleeping, He asked, "Couldst thou not watch one _____ with Me? Watch ye, and pray that ye enter not into temptation. The spirit indeed is willing, but the flesh is _____."

65. Peter cut off the ear of the high priest's servant, but Jesus healed it and said that all who take the sword shall _____ with the sword.

66. Our Lord asked, "Thinkest thou that I cannot ask My Father and He will give Me presently more than twelve legions of _____? The chalice which My Father hath given Me, shall I not _____ it?"

67. Jesus spoke to the crowd: "I sat daily with you, teaching in the Temple, and you laid not hands on Me. But this is your hour and the power of _____."

Matching

Directions: In each blank, write the letter of the phrase that correctly identifies that person, group, place or thing. Each blank is worth 1 point. 10 possible points.

1. ___ Judas

2. ___ Mary (sister of Martha & Lazarus)

3. ___ Paraclete

4. ___ kiss

5. ___ Malchus

6. ___ John

7. ___ reddish Paschal meal dish

8. ___ Gethsemani

9. ___ Jerusalem

10. ___ Herod

A) sign with which Judas betrayed Jesus
B) city Jesus wept over
C) apostle from Judea
D) prepared Paschal supper with Peter

E) reminder of bricks the Jews' ancestors made in Egypt
F) person Jesus called a fox
G) Holy Ghost

H) servant of high priest
I) poured ointment on Jesus' head
J) means olive press

Unit Eight
Section II
Subheadings 3 and 4

**3. The Redeemer Is Condemned to Death
4. The Redemption Is Accomplished**

Text
Pages
497-525

Perfect Score: 100   Score: _____

Completion

Directions: Complete and make each statement true and accurate by writing one or more words on each blank line. Each blank is worth 1 point. 90 possible points.

1. Jesus was brought to the palace of _____ , who questioned Him on His doctrine and His disciples.

2. A servant struck Jesus; He replied, "If I have spoken evil, give _____ of the evil, but if well, why strikest thou Me?"

3. The _____ let Peter in and asked him if he was a disciple of Jesus.

4. Later, a maidservant and then a servant who was a relative of _____ asked Peter if he was one of Jesus' disciples.

5. Peter said, "I know not this man of whom you speak"; when the cock crew (crowed), _____ turned and looked at Peter.

6. The Sanhedrin assembled in Caiphas' palace and held a trial, where many bore false _____ against Jesus.

7. Two witnesses remembered that Jesus had said He could rebuild the Temple of God in _____ days.

8. Jesus answered the high priest that He was the Son of God. Then Jesus said, "And you shall see the Son of Man sitting on the _____ hand of the power of God, and coming in the clouds of heaven."

9. The Sanhedrin could declare that a man was guilty of a crime punishable by death, but the power to order an execution belonged to the Roman _____ .

10. That night, the soldiers and the servants of the high priest blindfolded Our Lord, struck Him in the face and insulted Him, saying, "Prophesy unto us, O Christ, who is he that _____ thee?"

11. In the morning, the Sanhedrin said to Jesus again: "If Thou be the _____ , tell us."

12. Judas brought back the money he had been paid, saying, "I have sinned in betraying _____ blood."

13. In his despair, Judas rushed out and _____ himself with a halter.

14. The chief priests said it would not be lawful to put the money from Judas into the treasury because it was the price of _____ , so they used it to buy a _____ field, thus fulfilling the prophecy of Jeremias.

15. The members of the Sanhedrin remained outside in the Gabbatha of Pontius Pilate's palace because if they entered a heathen's house they would not be allowed to take part in the Feast of the _____ .

16. From his balcony Pilate said to the Jews, "Take you Him, and judge Him according to your _____ ."

17. When Pilate asked Jesus what He had done, Jesus answered, "If My Kingdom were of this _____ , My servants would certainly fight that I should not be delivered to the _____ ."

18. Our Lord told Pilate, "For this was I born, and for this cause I came into the world, that I should give _____ to the truth. Everyone that is of the truth, heareth My _____ ."

19. When Pilate heard that Jesus was from Galilee, he sent Him to _____ .

20. Jesus would not answer Herod's questions, so Herod ordered his soldiers to put a _____ garment upon Jesus to mock Him.

21. On solemn feast days, the governor released to the people one _____ chosen by them.

22. The crowd chose _____ to be released, instead of Jesus.

23. Pilate ordered his soldiers to strip Jesus of His garments, bind Him to a pillar, and _____ Him with cruel whips.

24. The soldiers put a _____ cloak upon Jesus, placed a crown of _____ on His head, put a reed in His hand and knelt before Him shouting, "Hail, _____ of the Jews!"

25. Pilate's _____ sent him a message, saying, "Have thou nothing to do with that _____ man; for I have suffered many things this day in a dream because of Him."

26. Pilate led Our bloody Savior before the crowd saying, "Behold the Man," but they only yelled, "_____ Him, _____ Him!"

27. The crowd told Pilate that Jesus ought to die because He made Himself the _____ .

28. Pilate asked Jesus, "Knowest Thou not that I have the power to _____ Thee, and I have the power to _____ Thee?" But Our Lord said, "Thou shouldst not have any power against Me unless it were given thee from above. Those that have delivered Me to thee have the greater _____ ."

29. Pilate finally surrendered to the will of the chief priests when they said that if he released Jesus, He would not be a friend of _____ .

30. Washing his hands before the people, Pilate said, "I am _____ of the blood of this just man; look you to it," and the mob answered, "His blood be upon us and upon our _____ !" The chief priests said, "We have no king but_____ ."

31. Jesus' body was bruised and torn and bleeding from the scourging; the soldiers put a _____ upon His shoulders and led Him away to be crucified.

32. The procession made its way to the hill of Calvary, also known as

_____ , a place where its barren shape gave it the
appearance of a skull.

33. The other two men who were crucified with Jesus were guilty of

_____ .

34. Our Lord became so weak while carrying the cross, after having endured so much cruelty before the procession had even begun, that He fell; the soldiers, being afraid that He would die before reaching Golgotha, forced

_____ of Cyrene to help Jesus carry His cross.

35. Some of the women began to weep loudly at the pitiable sight of Our Lord, but Jesus told them, "Daughters of Jerusalem, weep not over Me, but

weep for _____ , and for your _____ . For if in the green wood they do these things, what shall they do in the

_____ ?"

36. There is a tradition that Jesus came face to face with _____ ,

His _____ , and that a woman named

_____ offered Jesus a towel (or her veil) to wipe His face, and afterwards, the image of His sacred countenance was outlined upon it in blood.

37. There was a society of noble ladies who supplied a cup of wine mixed with

_____ to those who were to be crucified, but Jesus refused to drink it. The drink had the effect of making the person drowsy and deadening his

sense of _____ .

38. The board placed over Jesus' head read: "Jesus of Nazareth,

_____ of the Jews." Pilate had written this board for Jesus'

cross in Latin, _____ and _____ .

39. Our Lord prayed from the cross, "Father, _____ them, for they know not what they do."

40. The enemies of our Savior mocked Him saying, ". . . He trusted in God; let _____ now deliver Him" and, "If Thou be the King of the Jews, _____ Thyself."

41. Annas and _____ protested what Pilate wrote on the board over Jesus' head, but Pilate answered, "What I have written, I have _____ ."

42. The soldiers cast _____ to see who would get Jesus' seamless inner garment, thus fulfilling the Psalmist's words.

43. One of the robbers hanging with Jesus said to Him, "If Thou be the _____ , save Thyself and us," but the other robber rebuked him, telling him they were receiving their just punishment.

44. The "good thief" said to Jesus, "Lord, remember me when Thou shalt come into Thy _____ ," and Our Lord answered him, "This day thou shalt be with Me in _____ ."

45. The friends of Jesus who stood at the foot of His cross included His Mother Mary, Jesus' beloved disciple _____ , and Mary _____ .

46. To His Mother, Jesus said, "Woman, behold thy _____ ; and to John He said, "Behold thy _____ ."

47. In His hour of death, Jesus gave John and us His _____ , and John took her for his own.

48. Jesus had been nailed to the cross at about noon, and at _____ o'clock He cried out, "Eli, Eli, lamma sabacthani!" which means, "My God, my God, why hast Thou _____ Me?" When He said this, the people thought He was calling upon _____ .

49. When Our Lord said, "I thirst," a soldier held up a sponge soaked in _____ . Jesus, having drunk it, said, "It is _____ ," then, "Father, into Thy hands I commend My _____ ."

50. As soon as Jesus died, the _____ of the Temple in

Jerusalem was torn in two, the earth _____,

graves _____, and the dead came out of their

_____ .

51. The centurion in charge of the crucifixion said, "Indeed this man was

the _____ ."

52. When someone was crucified, if there was not enough time to let the person

hang until he died, the soldiers would break his _____
to cause him great agony before killing him with a sword or lance.

53. The soldiers saw no need to break any of Jesus' bones since He was already

dead, but one soldier pierced His side, and _____ and

_____ immediately flowed out.

54. Joseph, of the city of _____ , asked Pilate for the body of Jesus.

55. _____ joined Joseph in bringing myrrh and aloes; together
they placed the body of Jesus in a tomb and rolled a great stone across the door of
the tomb.

56. Mary Magdalen and a number of other _____ watched the
burial of Jesus.

57. The day after the crucifixion, the Pharisees and chief priests remembered

that Jesus had said, "After three days I will _____ again,"
so they asked Pilate to place a guard before Our Lord's sepulcher until the
third day so that His disciples would not steal His body and claim, "He is

_____ from the dead."

58. Pilate told the Pharisees they could guard the burial site of Jesus, so they

_____ the stone and set guards before it.

Matching

Directions: In each blank, write the letter of the phrase that correctly identifies that person, group, place or thing. Each blank is worth 1 point. 10 possible points.

1. ___ potter's field

2. ___ Annas

3. ___ Barabbas

4. ___ another name for Golgotha

5. ___ crucifixion

6. ___ strangulation

7. ___ Caiphas

8. ___ Joseph of Arimathea

9. ___ centurion

10. ___ Pontius Pilate

A) secret disciple of Jesus

B) a Jewish method of execution before Roman control

C) burying place for strangers

D) high priest

E) prisoner released to the Jews

F) Calvary

G) Roman governor

H) rode at head of procession to Golgotha

I) father-in-law of the high priest

J) Roman method of execution

Unit Eight
Section III

III. The Proof of Christ's Divinity

Text
Pages
526-546

Perfect Score: 100   Score: _____

Completion

Directions: Complete and make each statement true and accurate by writing one or more words on each blank line. Each blank is worth 1 point. 80 possible points.

1. The day after the Sabbath, there was an _____, and an
   angel descended from Heaven and rolled back the _____
   from Our Lord's tomb.

2. The guards at the tomb fainted with terror at the sight of the angel, whose
   countenance was as _____ .

3. _____ and Mary the Mother of James and
   _____ brought spices with which to anoint Jesus' body, but
   they found the stone rolled back and the body of the Lord Jesus gone.

4. Mary went back to the Cenacle where the apostles were gathered and told
   _____ and _____ that the body of Jesus
   had been taken.

5. The women saw a white-robed young man inside the _____
   who told them Jesus had risen and also told them to tell His disciples and Peter
   that Jesus "goeth before you into _____ ; there you shall see
   Him, as He told you."

6. Though _____ outran Peter in running to the sepulcher,
   he did not enter until Peter had arrived.

7. The napkin that had been tied about the _____ of Jesus
   lay folded up apart from the other linen cloths.

8. Returning to the sepulcher, Mary Magdalen saw two _____
   in the place where Jesus' body had been; they asked her why she was weeping.

9. Mary Magdalen answered, "Because they have taken away my

_____ , and I know not where they have

_____ Him."

10. When Jesus said to Mary Magdalen, " _____ ," she

recognized Him and answered, " _____ ," which means
"Master."

11. Our Lord told Mary Magdalen, "Do not _____ Me, for I am

not yet _____ to My Father. But go to My

_____ , and say to them: I ascend to My Father and to
your Father, to My God and your God."

12. The Sanhedrin paid the soldiers to tell the people that the

_____ of Jesus had come at night and

_____ His body when the soldiers were asleep.

13. Two disciples on their way to _____ met Jesus on the road,
although they did not recognize Him; they told Him how they had hoped Jesus

would be the one to redeem _____ .

14. When these disciples told the stranger (Jesus) of the things that had
happened concerning Jesus, He said to them, "Ought not Christ to

have _____ these things, and so to enter His

_____ ?"

15. Jesus explained to the two disciples all the things that the Scriptures had
foretold about Him, but they only recognized Him when at table with them, He

blessed the _____ , and _____ it and gave
it to them.

16. The two disciples said to each other, "Was not our heart

_____ within us, whilst He spoke in the way, and

opened to us the _____ ?"

17. Even though the doors to the Cenacle were locked, Jesus stood in the midst

of the Apostles and said to them, " _____ be to you."

18. The disciples thought they were seeing a ghost so Our Lord said, "See

My _____ and _____ , and know that it

is I Myself; handle, and see, for a spirit hath not _____

and _____ , as you see Me to have."

19. Jesus said to the disciples, "As the Father hath sent Me, I also

_____ you." Then Jesus _____ upon the

disciples and said, "Receive ye the _____ . Whose sins you

shall forgive, they are _____ them; whose sins you shall retain,

they are _____ ."

20. Since Thomas did not believe that the other Apostles had seen the Lord, Jesus
said to him the next time He came to the upper room, "Put in thy finger hither,
and see My hands; and bring hither thy hand, and put it into My

_____ ; and be not faithless, but _____ ."

21. At the sight of Jesus, Thomas cried out, "My _____ and
My God!"

22. "Because thou hast seen Me, Thomas, thou hast believed," said Jesus;

"blessed are they that have not _____ , and have

_____ ."

23. When the Apostles were fishing in Galilee, a man told them they would catch fish

if they cast the net on the _____ side of the ship.

24. _____ , realizing that the man who had called out to them
was the Lord, swam for the shore.

25. At Our Lord's command, Simon Peter drew the net to land, and the fishes in it

numbered _____ .

26. Jesus asked Peter, "Simon, son of John, _____ thou Me
more than these?" And when Peter said yes, the Lord told him, "Feed My

_____ ."

27. After Jesus asked Peter a second and a third time whether he loved Him, Peter was grieved and said, "Lord, Thou knowest _____ things; Thou knowest that I _____ Thee."

28. Our Lord said to Peter, "Feed My _____. Amen, amen, I say to thee, when thou wast _____, thou didst gird thyself, and didst walk where thou wouldst. But when thou shalt be _____, thou shalt stretch forth thy _____, and another shall gird thee, and lead thee whither thou wouldst not." With these words, Jesus prophesied that Peter would be _____ for His sake.

29. Our Lord spoke words that indicated that _____ would not die a martyr's death.

30. On a mountain in Galilee, Jesus said to the Apostles, "All power is given to Me in Heaven and in earth. Going, therefore, teach ye all _____; baptizing them in the name of the Father, and of the Son, and of the Holy Ghost; teaching them to observe all things whatsoever I have commanded you; and behold I am with you all _____, even to the _____ of the world. He that believeth and is baptized, shall be saved; but he that believeth not shall be _____ . . . ."

31. Forty days after Jesus rose from the dead, He told the Apostles they would soon be baptized with the _____ .

32. When the Apostles asked if Jesus would now restore the Kingdom of _____, He told them, "It is not for you to know the _____ or the _____ which the Father hath in His power."

33. Our Lord said, "All things must be fulfilled which are written in the Law of Moses, and in the prophets, and in the _____, concerning Me. Thus it is written and thus it behooved Christ to _____ , and to rise again from the dead the third day. And that _____ and the remission of sins should be preached in His name unto all _____ , beginning at Jerusalem."

34. Jesus led the Apostles out of the city toward _____ , and after blessing them, He rose up, and a _____ took Him out of their sight.

35. Two _____ appeared to the Apostles and said, "This Jesus Who was taken up from you into Heaven shall so come to you as you have seen Him going into Heaven."

36. The _____ and Mary Magdalen were two of the women who prayed in the Cenacle with the disciples and were present when the Holy Ghost came.

37. _____ was the new apostle to replace Judas Iscariot.

38. A sound as of a mighty _____ shook the whole house where the Apostles and disciples were gathered, and _____ of fire rested upon every one in the room, and they were all filled with the Holy Ghost.

39. The Holy Ghost gave the disciples the ability to speak different _____ .

40. The Apostles stood on the roof top and preached to the multitude; those in the crowd said to themselves, "Behold, are not all these that speak, _____ ? . . . we have heard them speak in our own tongues the wonderful works of God."

41. As Jesus had promised, the Apostles had the power to work _____ .

42. At first the Apostles preached only to the Jews, but later they made converts from among the _____ nations.

Matching

Directions: In each blank, write the letter of the phrase that correctly identifies that person, group, place or thing. Each blank is worth 2 points. 20 possible points.

1. ___ Cleophas

2. ___ Thomas

3. ___ Joseph Barsabas

4. ___ Feast of Pentecost

5. ___ priests

6. ___ bishops

7. ___ Mount of Olives

8. ___ Salome

9. ___ John

10. ___ Peter

A) also called the Just
B) Apostles' successors
C) disciple who met
   Jesus on the way
   to Emmaus
D) where Jesus
   ascended
   to Heaven

E) Apostle whom the
   others thought
   would not die
F) ordained to assist
   Apostles' ministry
G) went to help anoint
   Jesus' body

H) Holy Ghost
   descended
I) Apostle to whom
   Jesus gave duty of
   feeding His sheep
J) also called Didymus
   or Twin

ANSWER KEY

Completion — Part 1

1. serve	6. God	11. disciples	15. Old Testament;	18. fulfilled
2. will	7. supernatural	12. (Divine)	New Testament	19. prophetical
3. beautiful	8. Bible	Inspiration	16. contract;	20. prose
4. powerful	9. mysteries	13. truths; time	covenant	21. Tradition
5. loves	10. Divine Inspiration	14. Infallible	17. Redeemer; sins	

Completion — Part 2

1. NT 2. NT 3. OT 4. NT 5. OT 6. NT 7. OT 8. OT 9. OT 10. OT 11. OT 12. OT 13. NT
14. NT 15. NT 16. OT 17. OT 18. NT 19. OT 20. OT 21. NT 22. NT 23. NT 24. OT 25. OT

The Old Testament

Unit One   How God Came to Promise Man a Redeemer

Section I. The Story of Creation   (Workbook Pages 3-7)

Completion

1. existed	9. Him/God;	18. day; night	29. Mother; living	38. dust
2. beginning	themselves	19. third; Earth; Seas	30. Sanctifying Grace;	39. skins
3. God; equal	10. Lucifer	20. seventh; sanctified	holy; eternity	40. Cherubim; sword
4. truth; power;	11. Michael	21. image; likeness	31. die; Heaven	41. Original
happiness	12. Satan	22. slime; life	32. envied; loved	42. Blessed Virgin
5. nothing; needed;	13. Heaven	23. fishes; fowls;	33. Good; Evil	Mary
happiness	14. Genesis	earth; creature	34. God; opened; gods	
6. nine	15. six	24. Earthborn	35. Eve/the woman;	
7. Archangels;	16. twenty-four	25. Paradise; Eden	the serpent (or	
Cherubim;	17. beginning;	26. name	devil)	
Seraphim	Heaven; Earth;	27. ribs; woman	36. woman; seed; head	
8. Guardian	void; empty	28. bone; flesh	37. face; bread; earth	

Matching

1. F   2. H   3. D   4. C   5. B   6. J   7. I   8. A   9. G   10. E

Section II. The Descendants of Adam and Eve   (Workbook Pages 9-11)

Completion

1. sweat; bread;	4. Abel's; Cain's;	7. sin; pardoned;	11. tents;	14. Henoch; walked;
woman; sin	heart	findeth; kill	herdsmen	took
2. adored; burned;	5. Abel; brother;	8. sevenfold	12. Jubal	
sacrifice	keeper	9. mark; found;	13. Tubalcain;	
3. fruits; fields;	6. voice; blood;	kill	artificer;	
shepherd	earth; cursed	10. Seth; pleasing	brass; iron	

Matching

1. F   2. I   3. B   4. H   5. D   6. E   7. A   8. J   9. G   10. C

Section III. The Great Flood

Completion

1. disobedient; selfish; wicked
2. Sem; Cham; Japheth
3. flood; earth
4. 450; 75
5. 40; 40
6. dove; olive branch
7. altar; sacrifice
8. rainbow; destroy
9. Japheth; cloak
10. cursed; servant
11. tower; heaven
12. language; languages
13. Babel
14. Tigris; Euphrates
15. clay; cuneiform
16. Sargon; First
17. Code; Hammurabi
18. Babylonians; Egyptians
19. Hittites
20. Baal; Astarte

Matching

1. G   2. J   3. H   4. B   5. D   6. C   7. A   8. I   9. F   10. E

Unit Two   How God Founded the Nation from which The Redeemer of the World Came

Section I. Abraham, the Father of the Chosen People

(Workbook Pages 17-19)

Completion

1. Thare; Ur
2. Sarai; Chanaan
3. Jordan; Sodom
4. Chodorlahomor; Babylonia
5. Melchisedech; king
6. Melchisedech; bread; wine
7. Messias; Priest
8. count; stars; descendants
9. Agar; Ismael
10. wild; raised; tents
11. Abraham; Sara
12. slaves
13. God; angels
14. Sodom; Gomorrha
15. salt
16. 100; 90
17. heir
18. son; ram
19. children; obeyed
20. Rebecca; camels

Matching

1. E   2. G   3. J   4. I   5. F   6. H   7. A   8. B   9. C   10. D

Section II. God's Great Favors to Jacob

(Workbook Pages 21-23)

Completion

1. younger; older
2. birthright
3. Esau; hunt; bless
4. skins; kids
5. Jacob; Esau; Jacob
6. sword; serve; yoke
7. Chanaan
8. Esau; Jacob
9. ladder
10. sleepest; dust; blessed
11. seven; Rachel; Lia
12. seven; Rachael
13. injure; possessions
14. Esau; four
15. bless; Angel
16. Israel; strong
17. God; saved
18. altar; sacrifice
19. Benjamin
20. patriarch

Matching

1. H   2. G   3. J   4. D   5. B   6. I   7. A   8. E   9. C   10. F

Section III. The Children of Israel in Egypt

(Workbook Pages 25-29)

Completion

1. coat; colors
2. bowed
3. sun; moon; eleven
4. Ruben; pit
5. coat; wild beast
6. Egypt
7. Putiphar
8. wife; sin
9. branches; Pharao
10. baskets
11. butler; two; dreams
12. God
13. wheat; plenty; lean; famine
14. house; Pharao
15. governor; Egypt; knee
16. Nile; 18; famine
17. Putiphare; Aseneth
18. priest; social
19. one-fifth; plenty
20. Chanaan; Egypt; Benjamin
21. spies
22. Simeon; brother
23. joy; repented
24. money; paid
25. Benjamin; Juda
26. silver cup; Benjamin
27. slaves; death
28. Juda; Benjamin
29. God; Egypt; famine
30. Benjamin; clothing; 300
31. die; joy; face; alive
32. Gessen
33. Manasses; Ephraim
34. Juda; Expectation; Nations
35. Joseph; beautiful; St. Joseph
36. procession; Chanaan
37. Egypt; bones

Matching

1. H   2. G   3. B   4. C   5. A   6. I   7. J   8. E   9. D   10. F

170   BIBLE HISTORY — WORKBOOK

Section I. The Departure of the Israelites from Egypt (Workbook Pages 31-35)

Completion

1. Israelites
2. nomadic
3. idolatry; God
4. boy
5. tar; bulrushes; Nile
6. Pharao; Miriam; Hebrew
7. palace; prince
8. Israelites
9. overseer; killed
10. Madian; Mount Sinai
11. Jethro; Sephora
12. 40
13. bush; burn
14. shoes; feet; holy; Abraham; Isaac; Jacob
15. milk; honey
16. sacrifice
17. Am; Is
18. serpent
19. leprosy
20. blood
21. Aaron
22. Horeb
23. three; wilderness
24. straw
25. swallowed
26. hardened
27. frogs; fleas
28. finger
29. stoned
30. Gessen
31. boils; hail
32. men; women; children
33. darkness; flocks; victims
34. gold; silver
35. lamb; fourteenth
36. blood;
37. first-born; blood
38. Joseph
39. cloud; fire
40. rod; Red
41. manna
42. rock
43. Amalecites; rod
44. altar
45. judges; Jethro

(unnumbered) unleavened; wild; haste; Passing

Matching

1. F 2. H 3. I 4. G 5. D 6. B 7. C 8. J 9. A 10. E

Section II. The Revelation of God's Law on Mount Sinai (Workbook Pages 37-41)

Completion

1. two; Sinai
2. obedient; Chosen
3. three; boundary; death
4. name; vain
5. hear; die
6. Angel; Promised
7. Chanaan
8. blood; covenant
9. 40; 40
10. Aaron; calf
11. stone; golden calf
12. Lord; me
13. Levi; twenty-three thousand; penance
14. 40; 40; Commandments
15. horns; veil
16. Tabernacle; 45
17. Holy of Holies; Sanctuary
18. Court; 75; Holocausts
19. Laver
20. manna; rod
21. Mercy; Ark; Ark
22. six; Saturday; thanksgiving
23. Incense; Holocausts
24. Seven; Sanctuary
25. Aaron
26. Ephod; tribes
27. miter; Holy
28. Aaron; consecrated
29. Levi
30. duty; worship
31. unbloody
32. bloody
33. holocausts
34. peace; petition
35. Sabbatical
36. feast; worship
37. Atonement; Holy of Holies
38. Pasch; Nisan; lamb; unleavened
39. Pentecost; Sinai
40. Tabernacles
41. servile

Matching

1. D 2. F 3. A 4. J 5. B 6. I 7. C 8. E 9. G 10. H

Section III. The Wanderings of the Israelites in the Desert (Workbook Pages 43-46)

Completion

1. cloud; two
2. Levites; Ark of the Covenant
3. three; fire; repent
4. manna; quail
5. leprosy; seven
6. Cades; Chanaan
7. milk; honey; strong; cities; walls
8. possess; conquer
9. captain; Egypt
10. scouts; Josue; Caleb; Promised Land
11. 20; died
12. Amalecites; God
13. 250; priests; swallowed
14. Tabernacle; plague
15. bloomed; priesthood; Moses
16. speak
17. rock; Promised Land
18. Cades; Seir
19. Hor; Eleazar; Aaron; thirty
20. Wilderness; Sin; serpents
21. serpent; struck; live
22. Amorrhites; capital
23. Gad; Ruben; Manasses
24. Josue; Ephraim; military
25. Nebo; Promised Land; 120
26. grave; adore; idolatry
27. Moab; Angel
28. Balaam; curse; three; blessing
29. speak; commandeth
30. Star; Jacob; scepter; Israel; rule

Matching

1. H 2. F 3. D 4. J 5. A 6. I 7. B 8. C 9. G 10. E

Section IV. Josue, the Commander of the Israelites (Workbook Pages 47-51)

Completion

1. Phoenicia;
   Mediterranean;
   Arabia; center
2. fountains;
   pomegranates;
   olive; honey
3. Maryland
4. flocks; herds
5. Carmel; Jordan
6. rainy; dry
7. Philistines; Minos;
   Crete
8. Palestine;
   Philistines
9. iron; alphabet
10. Syrians; nomad
11. Lot; Dead;
    Moabites
12. false gods; High;
    true
13. eagle; stars; wise;
    understanding;
    Esau; Esau
14. Basan; Galaad
15. Amorrhites;
    abominations
16. sword; sling
17. Rahab;
    Jericho;
    scarlet
18. Jordan; river;
    dry path
19. monument
20. Galgal; manna
21. Angel; sword
22. Forty; six
23. seventh; Ark;
    Covenant; seven
24. Shout; city
25. trumpets
26. disobedience;
    Achan; plunder
27. ambush
28. Gabaon
29. sun; moon
30. Asor
31. Levites; priests
32. east
33. idolatry; stone;
    Silo
34. Thamnath Saraa
35. Eleazar; high
    priest
36. Jacob

Matching

1. E 2. I 3. H 4. F 5. A 6. G 7. D 8. C 9. J 10. B

Section V. The Israelites in the Promised Land (Workbook Pages 53-55)

Completion

1. patriarchal
2. pagan
3. Judge
4. Judges
5. altar; Baal
6. Madianites
7. dew; dry
8. dry; dew
9. three
10. Gedeon; Lord
11. Silo; idolatry
12. army; strength
13. father-in-law
14. gates
15. Dalila; hair
16. hair; pillars
17. lent
18. Ophni; Phinees
19. servant
20. negligence
21. Philistines; Ark of
    the Covenant
22. Heli
23. Dagon
24. mice; boils
25. oxen; priest
26. Fifty
27. worship
28. Philistines

Matching

1. F 2. E 3. H 4. J 5. B 6. A 7. C 8. I 9. D 10. G

Section VI. The Story of Ruth (Workbook Pages 57-59)

Completion

1. famine;
   Bethlehem;
   Noemi; Moab
2. Moabite;
   Orpha; Ruth
3. ten
4. Noemi; Juda
5. mother; mercy;
   departed
6. people; people;
   God; God;
   death
7. relative
8. Booz; glean
9. Moses; second;
   grain; poor
10. gleaned; evening;
    flour; Noemi
11. Booz;
    kindness;
    mother-in-law
12. protect; noon
13. house; Obed
14. Noemi
15. Obed; King;
    Savior

Matching

1. E 2. F 3. J 4. B 5. H 6. I 7. C 8. A 9. G 10. D

Unit Four How God's Chosen People Lived under Their Kings

Section I. Saul, the First King of the Israelites

(Workbook Pages 61-65)

Completion

1. God; human
2. Saul; king
3. Gabaa; animals
4. oil; anointed; deliver
5. Maspha; lots
6. Saul
7. oxen; Ammonites
8. Jabes Galaad
9. Ammonites; Madianites
10. Galgal
11. Philistines
12. kingship; family
13. king; ornaments; flocks
14. holocausts; obedience; sacrifices; word
15. Isai
16. youngest; David
17. Spirit
18. harp; armor bearer
19. Goliath; nine
20. marriage; Goliath
21. brothers
22. Philistine; reproach
23. sling; stones
24. head; Philistine; God
25. thousands; tens; thousands
26. Jonathan
27. Saul
28. hundred; Merob
29. 200; Merob; Michol
30. tomorrow; die
31. statue; goat skin
32. four; Philistines; envy
33. Engaddi; killed; hate
34. Ziph; spear
35. sinned; harm
36. witch/fortune teller
37. David; obey; Israel; me
38. head; Astarte; Bethsan
39. woods
40. Jonathan

Matching

1. E   2. I   3. G   4. B   5. F   6. H   7. J   8. D   9. C   10. A

Section II. The King from Whom the Redeemer Descended

(Workbook Pages 67-70)

Completion

1. Hebron; Juda
2. Abner; Hebron
3. Chanaanites; lame; blind
4. Joab
5. capital; David
6. Tyre; Philistines; Lebanon
7. Cariathiarim; Oza
8. priests
9. Levite; three
10. robes; Levites; Tabernacle
11. revolt
12. Hebron; vow
13. palace; Chusai; Jordan
14. Galaad
15. hair
16. Joab; heart
17. Urias; front
18. Nathan; lamb
19. sin; die; die
20. Solomon
21. temple; Solomon
22. one thousand; one thousand; one thousand
23. David
24. Philistines
25. fighting
26. iron-pointed; iron-pointed
27. citizens'; standing
28. 33
29. Levites; civil; judges
30. officers; heads
31. grain
32. wine; oil; valleys
33. Ark; treasures; choir; sacred
34. feast; Psalms; sufferings
35. Saul
36. nothing; shadow; death
37. king; prophet; forty
38. penitents; repentance
39. kingdom; Kingdom; Messias

Matching

1. I   2. H   3. J   4. G   5. B   6. E   7. A   8. F   9. D   10. C

Section III. The Israelites under King Solomon

(Workbook Pages 71-74)

Completion

1. twenty
2. one thousand; Gabaa
3. wisdom; wealth; glory; life
4. half; child; kill; mine; thine; divide
5. Proverbs; Ecclesiastes
6. queen; God; pleased; throne
7. firs; cedars
8. building; fourth; seven
9. Tabernacle; east
10. Gentiles; Israelites; Priests
11. Holy Place; Incense; Candlesticks
12. Holies; Ark of the Covenant
13. Levites; Tabernacles
14. oxen; sheep; fire; consume
15. protect
16. one
17. four; Forest; Libanus; gold
18. Euphrates; Egypt
19. 40; golden; Israel
20. Tadmor; East
21. Hiram; commerce
22. gold; silver
23. meat; grain; palace
24. 12; tribes
25. God; united
26. taxes/taxation; idolatry; pagan
27. fortifications; Ephraim; Benjamin
28. twelve; Solomon; ten; one; David; gods
29. Jeroboam; Egypt; kill
30. Jerusalem

Matching

1. G   2. H   3. F   4. A   5. I   6. J   7. B   8. C   9. D   10. E

ANSWER KEY   173

Section IV. The Division of Solomon's Kingdom (Workbook Pages 75-77)

Completion

1. Sichem; forty-one
2. taxes
3. counselors
4. heavy
5. heavy; add; whips; scorpions
6. Jerusalem; Semeias
7. Benjamin; Juda
8. Israel
9. Levites
10. calves
11. priest; sacrifice
12. Sichem; patriotism
13. Thersa
14. Josias
15. withered; altar
16. Abia
17. gods; rooted; son; Assyrians
18. Jeroboam
19. altar; idolatry
20. Sesac
21. Assyria; Babylonia
22. agriculture
23. seventeen; Abiam
24. Asa; ten

Matching

1. H   2. I   3. A   4. E   5. B   6. J   7. C   8. D   9. F   10. G

Section V. Holy Servants of God—Their Preaching and Miracles (Workbook Pages 79-83)

Completion

1. Amri; Samaria
2. Baal; Jezabel
3. drought
4. raven
5. less; rain
6. son
7. rain
8. Abdias; one hundred
9. Carmel
10. fire
11. Baal
12. talking; journey
13. twelve
14. Israel; servant
15. fire; God
16. death
17. angel; forty; Horeb
18. Syria; Jehu; Eliseus
19. violent; blasphemy
20. falsely; vineyard
21. blood; Jezabel; Israel
22. haircloth
23. Micheas
24. chariot
25. Joram; Israel; Jezabel
26. Josaphat
27. spirit; seest
28. chariot; horses; waters
29. seven; leprosy
30. miracles
31. Edomites
32. simple; evil
33. gave; taken away; Blessed
34. trust; Redeemer; skin; God
35. seven; three
36. Nineve; ship
37. lots; sea
38. belly; three; three
39. 40; Nineve
40. fast; sackcloth
41. mercy
42. Resurrection; three; three; three; three

Matching

1. F   2. G   3. H   4. I   5. B   6. A   7. J   8. C   9. D   10. E

Unit Five   How God's Chosen People Were Led into Captivity and Their Kingdom Was Destroyed

Section I. The Assyrian Invasions (Workbook Pages 85-88)

Completion

1. poor
2. poor; Assyrians
3. Samaria
4. Media; Jerusalem
5. death
6. property
7. swallow
8. poor; much; cheerfully; pride
9. debt
10. liver
11. Sara
12. Gabelus
13. gall
14. Raphael
15. Nineve; Captivity
16. Jerusalem
17. Levites
18. seven; David
19. Isaias
20. fifteen; Assyrians
21. Egypt
22. Sennacherib
23. 185,000
24. Babylon
25. water; five
26. limit
27. Holofernes; soldiers
28. Judith; Bethulia
29. Manasses

Matching

1. B   2. G   3. I   4. A   5. H   6. C   7. J   8. E   9. F   10. D

Section II. The Babylonian Captivity

(Workbook Pages 89-93)

Completion

1. God; Egypt
2. Jerusalem; sacred vessels
3. Babylon
4. son
5. Temple; soldiers; workman
6. Sedecias
7. yoke
8. fourth; Jeremias; Babylonians
9. Temple
10. Jeremias
11. Lamentations
12. Hanging Gardens
13. Daniel; Azarias
14. Ezechiel
15. Susanna; death; sin; Lord
16. Daniel; truth; Israel
17. mastic; holm
18. wise-men
19. God
20. governor; burdens; freedom
21. sacrifices; synagogues
22. Ananias; Misael; Azarias
23. angel
24. Evil-Merodach; lions
25. Habacuc; Daniel; pottage
26. persecutors
27. vessels; Nabuchodonosor
28. Mane; Thecel; Phares
29. Thecel
30. Phares; Medes
31. purple; gold; third
32. Cyrus
33. please
34. major
35. Isaias
36. enemies; themselves
37. Cyrus; Persians
38. Jesse; flower; understanding; fortitude; godliness
39. virgin
40. Church; nations; Gentiles
41. Jeremias
42. parables; Evangelists
43. Daniel; Savior

Matching

1. I   2. E   3. H   4. F   5. C   6. A   7. B   8. J   9. D   10. G

Section III. The Jews in Babylon and Persia under Cyrus

(Workbook Pages 95-97)

Completion

1. Egypt
2. sacred vessels
3. 70
4. Assyrians
5. Zorobabel
6. sacrifice
7. idolaters
8. Zacharias
9. 515
10. Esther; uncle
11. Aman; Mardochai
12. massacre; revolt
13. three
14. banquet; death
15. gibbet; Mardochai
16. historians; history
17. Mardochai
18. Aman; robes
19. Aman
20. gibbet; death
21. Artaxerxes I; rites
22. pagan
23. Scriptures
24. Nehemias
25. family
26. Tobias; vessels
27. poor
28. chief priest
29. schismatical; Samaritans

Matching

1. F   2. I   3. J   4. H   5. G   6. C   7. D   8. B   9. E   10. A

Section IV. The Last Days of the Kingdom of Juda

(Workbook Pages 99-103)

Completion

1. Persians
2. Moses; Samaria; Garizim
3. Greek; Persians
4. Alexander; Jerusalem
5. dream
6. conscience
7. four
8. overseer; treasury; sacrifices; King
9. Onias; widows; orphans
10. soldier; golden; scourged
11. sacrifice; recovery
12. Onias
13. Epiphanes; Syria; slaves; Treasury; unclean
14. Temple; death
15. slavery; strangers
16. strong; martyrdom
17. Eleazar; swine
18. die; disobey; fathers
19. God
20. judgment; seeth; pain; eternal
21. Mathathias; five
22. Machabeus; Temple; consecrated; eight
23. Edomites; Ammonites; Philistines; refugees
24. votive offerings
25. sacrifice; sins; wholesome; dead; sin
26. Jerusalem; sincere
27. Eupator; Alcimus
28. Onias; Jeremias; 3,000; Nicaner; Syrian
29. Rome, Laisa
30. Simon
31. Jews
32. civil; Herod; Jacob; Juda; Expectation; Savior

Matching

1. E   2. I   3. F   4. H   5. A   6. C   7. J   8. B   9. G   10. D

The New Testament

Section I. Preparation of the World for the Messias

(Workbook Pages 107-111)

Completion

1. Maryland
2. Galilee; Jordan
3. Sebaste
4. Samaria
5. Perea
6. Decapolis; Roman
7. Julius Caesar; Jew; cruelty
8. Archelaus; Antipas; Philip
9. Archelaus; procurator; festivals
10. publicans; traitors
11. denarius; twenty
12. twenty-four hundred
13. Jewish
14. Josue
15. veils; turban
16. stones; one
17. cushions; fingers
18. feet
19. fishing; cattle; farming
20. nine; six
21. ownership
22. Purim; Dedication
23. chief priests; high priest
24. religious; sentence; procurator's
25. Temple; synagogues
26. excommunicated
27. Scribes
28. Pharisees
29. error
30. letter
31. phylacteries
32. Sadducees; body
33. Sadducees; feared
34. Essenes; zeal
35. Nazarites; mortification
36. Judea; cultured; dialect
37. Garizim; Moses
38. Judea; Galilee
39. Aramaic; Greek; Hebrew; Latin
40. Herod; Herod
41. Holy; Holies
42. Israelites; Women
43. Gentiles; abuse
44. Pinnacle

Matching

1. E   2. A   3. F   4. B   5. J   6. H   7. I   8. G   9. D   10. C

Section II. The Redeemer among Men

(Workbook Pages 113-119)

Completion

1. Gabriel
2. speak/talk
3. handmaid
4. Magnificat
5. magnify
6. prophet
7. Joseph; virgin; Emmanuel
8. census
9. manger
10. Savior
11. good will
12. circumcised
13. turtledoves
14. Simeon
15. resurrection; sword
16. Anna
17. star
18. frankincense; Herod
19. two; Rachael; comforted
20. Egypt
21. Nazareth
22. Pasch
23. 12
24. doctors of the law
25. Father
26. 30; Joseph
27. locusts
28. penance
29. wilderness; straight
30. baptized
31. water; fire
32. pleased
33. bread
34. bread
35. tempt
36. kingdoms; serve
37. Lamb
38. Andrew
39. Cephas
40. Nazareth
41. fishers
42. Matthew
43. devils
44. Herodias
45. lepers; poor; prophet
46. Salome
47. John the Baptist
48. Nicodemus; Holy Ghost
49. tears
50. Simon
51. whole
52. Martha
53. best
54. laborers
55. three
56. synagogue
57. Isaias; spirit; anointed
58. prophet
59. Mount
60. life
61. speak
62. knock
63. refresh; humble
64. Mary
65. miracle
66. Zacheus; lost
67. Jacob
68. Jews
69. fountain
70. Messias; speaking
71. will
72. Savior

Matching

1. I   2. F   3. G   4. H   5. J   6. B   7. C   8. D   9. E   10. A

Section I. Christ, the Great Teacher   (Workbook Pages 121-127)

Completion

1. pleasure
2. parables
3. heart
4. birds
5. Kingdom of God
6. mother
7. plow
8. scattereth; Mammon
9. Lazarus; Hell
10. brothers; Moses
11. Moses
12. secret
13. men; secret
14. sinner
15. humbled; exalted
16. rest; sinful
17. man; man
18. Bethsaida
19. work
20. life
21. Abraham
22. holy
23. Son
24. Husbandmen; son
25. vineyard
26. Gentiles; business
27. thieves
28. body
29. explained
30. Love; pray
31. publicans; merciful
32. 70
33. torturers
34. right; left; cloak
35. judged; beam
36. them
37. hardness; asunder
38. Samaritan
39. faith
40. doubt
41. Father; Peace; David; justice
42. Jews
43. God; men
44. deny; cross; lose; find; soul
45. mother
46. chalice
47. servant; minister
48. Samaritans; burn
49. destroy
50. for
51. children; enter
52. scandalize; millstone; sea; angels
53. Messias
54. James; snow; sun
55. Moses; Elias
56. tabernacles; Son
57. risen

Matching

1. B   2. I   3. F   4. H   5. C   6. G   7. A   8. J   9. D   10. E

Section II. Christ, the Friend of the Poor and the Sick   (Workbook Pages 129-135)

Completion

1. carpenter
2. Nazareth
3. home; charity
4. poor in spirit
5. world
6. glory; good
7. Commandments
8. poor; follow
9. riches; camel
10. impossible; possible
11. tribes
12. hundredfold; life everlasting
13. more; abundance; want
14. Soul
15. scandalize
16. covetousness
17. friends
18. everlasting
19. riches; sin
20. poor
21. judgment seat
22. love
23. external
24. Son of Man
25. sheep
26. blessed; stranger; visited; came
27. least; Me
28. punishment
29. worthy; word; healed
30. roof
31. forgive
32. hem
33. whole
34. David
35. power; visible
36. Light
37. Siloe
38. Sabbath
39. believe
40. ears; tongue
41. Baptism
42. Unclean; unclean
43. priest
44. ten
45. glory
46. sin
47. Holy One
48. legion
49. swine
50. unbelief
51. unbelief
52. mustard seed; mulberry; obey; fasting
53. children; dogs
54. courage
55. Naim
56. Jairus; sleepeth
57. Talitha cumi
58. resurrection; live; forever
59. four
60. expedient; die; perish
61. Savior
62. doctrine
63. Lazarus

Matching

1. F   2. D   3. J   4. B   5. I   6. A   7. C   8. E   9. H   10. G

(Workbook Pages 137-142)

Completion

1. Church
2. Church
3. Simon Peter (or Peter); net
4. men
5. flesh; rock; Church; keys; bind; loose
6. error; law
7. parables
8. vine; husbandman
9. fruit; itself; nothing
10. shepherd
11. life
12. shepherd; life; fold
13. hireling
14. Son of Man; devil; angels
15. fire; gnashing
16. wicked; just
17. mustard
18. field; pearl
19. sacrifice
20. Church; holy
21. fig
22. graces
23. one
24. faithful; faithful; joy
25. ten; given; taken away
26. seed; temptation; riches; patience
27. Christ
28. thief
29. hour; hour
30. foolish; oil; bridegroom
31. day
32. Son of God; delights
33. Church; head
34. happy; Heaven
35. Eucharist
36. five
37. loaves; fishes
38. twelve
39. king
40. loaves; perisheth; everlasting
41. believe
42. Life; dead; Living; flesh; life
43. flesh; blood; raise; forever
44. hard
45. spirit
46. Father
47. Simon Peter; eternal; Christ

Matching

1. E   2. J   3. H   4. I   5. A   6. C   7. B   8. F   9. G   10. D

Unit Eight   How Christ Redeemed the World and Returned to Heaven

Section I. Christ, the Savior of Mankind   (Workbook Pages 143-146)

Completion

1. Paschal; sin
2. sacrifices; debt
3. Kingdom of Heaven
4. body; come; will
5. sinners
6. ninety-nine
7. penance; penance
8. coins
9. angels; penance
10. Heaven; servants
11. calf; commandments
12. with; thine; dead; life; lost; found
13. householder; penny
14. just
15. eleventh
16. penny
17. wrong; penny; last
18. adultery; stoned
19. write; sin; stone
20. condemn; sin

Matching

1. I   2. G   3. A   4. H   5. C   6. J   7. B   8. F   9. D   10. E

Section II: The Passion and Death of Christ

Subheadings 1 and 2: The Enemies of Christ Plot against Him   (Workbook Pages 147-154)
Christ Institutes the Holy Eucharist

Completion

1. Jerusalem
2. faith
3. prosperity
4. blasphemy
5. blaspheming
6. works
7. heareth
8. glory; death
9. day
10. I am
11. Moses
12. John the Baptist
13. speak; common
14. hear
15. Mary
16. poor
17. poor; burial
18. colt
19. King; meek
20. palm; Blessed
21. stones
22. children; chickens
23. enemies; stone
24. infants
25. Gentiles
26. race
27. fruit; lose; keepeth
28. name; again
29. prince; Myself
30. mountain
31. authority; baptism
32. emperor
33. God; God
34. son
35. Judas (Iscariot)
36. thirty
37. Paschal
38. desire
39. vine
40. serveth
41. feet
42. lord
43. born
44. John
45. dipped; quickly
46. Body
47. Blood; sins
48. commemoration; Blood
49. sacrifice; oblation
50. disciples
51. strike
52. confirm
53. Peter
54. mansions
55. truth
56. Philip
57. commandments; Spirit
58. orphans
59. teach
60. friends; name
61. hour; Thee
62. death
63. chalice; blood
64. hour; weak
65. perish
66. angels; drink
67. darkness

Matching

1. C   2. I   3. G   4. A   5. H   6. D   7. E   8. J   9. B   10. F

Subheadings 3 and 4: The Redeemer Is Condemned to Death
The Redemption Is Accomplished

Completion

1. Annas
2. testimony
3. portress
4. Malchus
5. Jesus
6. witness
7. three
8. right
9. governor
10. struck
11. Christ
12. innocent
13. hanged
14. blood; potter's
15. Passover
16. law
17. world; Jews
18. testimony; voice
19. Herod (Antipas)
20. white
21. prisoner
22. Barabbas
23. scourge
24. purple; thorns; King
25. wife; just
26. Crucify; crucify
27. Son of God
28. crucify; release; sin
29. Caesar
30. innocent; children; Caesar
31. cross
32. Golgotha
33. robbery
34. Simon
35. yourselves; children; dry
36. Mary; mother; Veronica
37. myrrh; pain
38. King; Greek; Hebrew
39. forgive
40. God; save
41. Caiphas; written
42. lots
43. Christ
44. Kingdom; Paradise
45. John; Magdalen
46. son; Mother
47. Mother
48. three; forsaken; Elias
49. vinegar; finished; spirit
50. veil; quaked; opened; tombs
51. Son of God
52. legs
53. blood; water
54. Arimathea
55. Nicodemus
56. women
57. rise; risen
58. sealed

Matching

1. C   2. I   3. E   4. F   5. J   6. B   7. D   8. A   9. H   10. G

Section III: The Proof of Christ's Divinity

Completion

1. earthquake; stone
2. lightning
3. Mary Magdalen; Salome
4. Peter; John
5. sepulcher; Galilee
6. John
7. head
8. Angels
9. Lord; laid
10. Mary; Rabboni
11. touch; ascended; brethren
12. disciples; stolen
13. Emmaus; Israel
14. suffered; glory
15. bread; broke
16. burning; Scriptures
17. Peace
18. hands; feet; flesh; bones
19. send; breathed; Holy Ghost; forgiven; retained
20. side; believing
21. Lord
22. seen; believed
23. right
24. Peter
25. 153
26. lovest; lambs
27. all; love
28. sheep; younger; old; hands; crucified
29. John
30. nations; days; consummation; condemned
31. Holy Ghost
32. Israel; times; moments
33. psalms; suffer; penance; nations
34. Bethania; cloud
35. Angels
36. Blessed Virgin Mary
37. Matthias
38. wind; tongues
39. languages
40. Galileans
41. miracles
42. Gentile

Matching

1. C   2. J   3. A   4. H   5. F   6. B   7. D   8. G   9. E   10. I

WONDERFUL CATHOLIC HISTORY TEXTS

CHRIST THE KING—LORD OF HISTORY

Anne W. Carroll   No. 1228
ISBN: 978-0-89555-503-8 $24.00

474 Pp. PB. Index. A fast-paced, highly readable, interesting Catholic world history for high schools and adult reading. Used by Seton Home Study School for 10th Grade. Covers the development of Western Civilization from a Catholic perspective. Shows Christ and His Church to be the center of *all* history.

CHRIST THE KING, LORD OF HISTORY—WORKBOOK AND STUDY GUIDE
Belinda T. Mooney
No. 1754   ISBN: 978-0-89555-673-8 $21.00
192 Pp. PB. Over 50 Questions for each of the 30 Chapters.

SET: CHRIST THE KING TEXTBOOK AND WORKBOOK
No. 1766 $36.00

THE OLD WOIRLD AND AMERICA

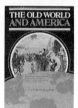

Most Rev. Philip J. Furlong   No. 1002
ISBN: 978-0-89555-202-0 $21.00

384 Pp. PB. Impr. 200 Illus. A famous world history text geared for the 5th thru 8th grades. Guides the student from Creation through the early exploration of the New World. Will help develop great respect for the Catholic Church. Contains Study Questions, Activities, Illustrations, Maps, Index, etc.

THE OLD WORLD AND AMERICA—ANSWER KEY
No. 1550   ISBN: 978-0-89555-620-2 $10.00
96 Pp. PB. Answer Key for the above book.

SET: THE OLD WORLD AND AMERICA TEXTBOOK AND ANSWER KEY   No. 1854 $27.00

BIBLE HISTORY

Fr. George Johnson, Fr. Jerome Hannan and Sr. M. Dominica   No. 1776
ISBN: 978-0-89555-692-9 $24.00

558 Pp. PB. Impr. This is our best Bible History Textbook for 8th-12th grade. The format is highly readable, fast-paced and interesting. Contains study questions by chapter, maps, illustrations and comprehensive Index. Covers both the Old and New Testament.

CHRIST AND THE AMERICAS

Anne W. Carroll   No. 1387
ISBN: 978-0-89555-594-6 $24.00

440 Pp. PB. Index. This great Catholic high school history text beautifully weaves together North, Central and South American history from a Catholic perspective. Covers the earliest explorers through the 1990's. Used by Seton Home Study School for 11th Grade. Fascinating insights not found elsewhere.

CHRIST AND THE AMERICAS—WORKBOOK AND STUDY GUIDE
Belinda T. Mooney
No. 1884   ISBN: 978-0-89555-744-5 $21.00
192 Pp. PB. Over 50 Questions for each of the 30 Chapters.

SET: CHRIST AND THE AMERICAS TEXTBOOK AND WORKBOOK   No. 1921 $36.00

OUR PIONEERS AND PATRIOTS

Most Rev. Philip J. Furlong   No. 1396
ISBN: 978-0-89555-592-2 $24.00

505 Pp. PB. Impr. 235 Illus. & maps. Index. Well-known 5th-8th grade American History text with Study Questions & Activities. Covers Saints, historic figures and events as well as the role of Catholics in the development of America. Includes Columbus, St. Isaac Jogues, Fr. Marquette and Mother Seton, etc.

OUR PIONEERS AND PATRIOTS—ANSWER KEY
No. 1529   ISBN: 978-0-89555-606-6 $10.00
96 Pp. PB. Answer Key for the above book.

SET: OUR PIONEERS AND PATRIOTS TEXTBOOK AND ANSWER KEY   No. 1855 $29.00

BIBLE HISTORY—WORKBOOK

BIBLE HISTORY—WORKBOOK
Marie Ignatz   No. 1792
ISBN: 978-0-89555-703-2 $21.00
179 Pp. PB. Great for classwork, tests or personal study.

SET: BIBLE HISTORY TEXTBOOK AND WORKBOOK
No. 1819 $35.00